SUPER INVENTION FAIR PROJECTS

By Dr. Zondra Knapp
Illustrated by Chris Sabatino

LOWELL HOUSE JUVENILE

LOS ANGELES

NTC/Contemporary Publishing Group

To the best lil' inventors in the whole wide world: Frederick & Alexander Knapp
—"Dr. Zee" Z.L.L.K.

Published by Lowell House
A Division of NTC/Contemporary Publishing Group, Inc.
4255 West Touhy Avenue, Lincolnwood (Chicago), Illinois 60712 U.S.A.
Copyright © 2000 by NTC/Contemporary Publishing Group, Inc.

Managing Director and Publisher: Jack Artenstein
Director of Publishing Services: Rena Copperman
Editorial Director: Brenda Pope-Ostrow
Director of Art Production: Bret Perry
Project Editor: Jessica Oifer
Designer: Treesha Runnells-Vaux

Lowell House books can be purchased at special discounts
when ordered in bulk for premiums and special sales.
Contact Customer Service at the address above, or call 1-800-323-4900.

Printed and bound in the United States of America

DHD 10 9 8 7 6 5 4 3 2 1

Library of Congress Cataloging-in-Publication Data

Knapp, Zondra Lewis.
  Super invention fair projects / by Dr. Zee (Zondra) Knapp; illustrated by Chris Sabatino.
    p. cm.
  Summary: Examines invention fairs, which display unique inventions from young
people across the country, discusses what an invention is and how to develop one, and
introduces some inventors and their achievements.
  ISBN 0-7373-0315-8 (alk. Paper)
  1. Inventions—Competitions—Juvenile literature. [1. Inventions. 2. Inventors.] I.
Sabatino, Chris, ill. II. Title.

T339 .K68 2000
607'.73—dc21

99-043743

CONTENTS

Foreword: Who Is an Inventor? 6

Chapter 1: Great Inventors

The Characteristics of an Inventor 8
What Makes a Great Inventor? 9
What Is an Invention? 10
Famous Inventions and Their Inventors 11
Women and Minority Inventors 13

Chapter 2: Getting Started

What Is an Invention Fair Project? 18
The Seven Steps to Inventing 19
Choosing a Great Idea 23
Evaluating Your Idea 25
Invention Categories 26
Invention or Innovation? 29

Chapter 3: The Inventor's Journal

What Is a Journal? 31
Types of Journals 32
Witnessing Your Journal 33

Chapter 4: Planning Your Project

A Project Timeline 38
The Six-Week Plan 39

Chapter 5: Research and Resources

What Is Research? 42
Primary vs. Secondary Research 43
Books and Magazines 45
The Internet 47
The Experts 49

Chapter 6: Designing Your Project

Drawings and Sketches 55
Subtractive Designs 56
Additive Designs 57

Chapter 7: Materials, Supplies, and Tools

Your Junkpile 58
Common Supplies and Tools 63
Scientific Supply Houses 64

Chapter 8: Building Your Project

Finding a Workplace 66
The Stages of Construction .67
Quantitative Measuring 68
Qualitative Measuring 70
Playing It "Safe" 70

Chapter 9: Getting Ready for the Fair

The Invention Fair 76
The Entry Form 77
The Judges 78
Judging Forms and Scoring .78
Invention Fair Displays 82
Oral Presentations 84
Certificate of Participation .86

Chapter 10: Patents and Trademarks

What Is a Patent? 87
Types of Patents 87
Filing for a Patent 91
Trademarking Your Name 93

Appendix:

Invention Contests and Competitions 94

Index

Index 96

Acknowledgments

I would like to thank the following people for their help with this book: Stanley Mason, the premier small-product inventor in the United States, for his help and encouragement; Dr. George Margolin for his invaluable advice on inventing; Dr. LaMoine Motz, Past President of the National Science Teachers Association (NSTA); Dr. Gary Nelson, President of Edison's Inventors Association, for his support and use of materials in the booklet titled "Edison Young Inventors Program Resource"; Frankie Cox, Public Affairs Officer of the United States Patent and Trademark Office; Joann Uslick, Camp Invention, National Inventors Hall of Fame; and Joyce Keene, section author of New Hampshire Young Inventor's Program Teacher Guide titled "Meant to Invent."

In addition, I want to thank all the amazing young inventors featured in this book: Diana Alvarez, Joel Adam Blondy, Trisha Buss, Joshua Gonzales, Ali Kaslow, Doug Krailo, Elizabeth Low, Charlie Matykiewicz, Grace Reynolds, Allison Sacco, and Leora H. Saviano, and all their parents and teachers, who helped them prepare their submissions.

Lastly, special thanks to all those other kid inventors in the Santa Ana Unified School District's Science and Invention Fair, the Tustin and Irvine Unified School Districts' Invention Fairs, the Orange County Science and Engineering Fair, the California State Science Fair, the National Inventive and Creative Thinking Contest (sponsored by the National Inventive Thinking Association), and the International Invention Convention.

Foreword: Who Is an Inventor?

by Stanley Mason, premier inventor and president and CEO of SIMCO Inc.

A long time ago . . . when I was very young . . . I made an invention. I wasn't trying to make one. It just happened.

I was seven years old, and I asked my father for 15 cents to buy some minnows [tiny fish used for bait] to go fishing. He turned me down. He said that fishing wasn't a good use of my time, and that he would keep his 15 cents.

My mother overheard this conversation and asked me why I couldn't make my own minnow. She suggested I make one that would last a long time so I would not have to ask my father for any money. She then gave me a wooden clothespin, the kind that anyone could buy at the market or hardware store.

I noticed how close the clothespin was to the size of a minnow and how easily I could carve it into the shape of a minnow. I added a hook to one end and an eye to the other. I was so excited about my creation that I immediately went fishing. I cast my artificial minnow into the water. It attracted some fish, but none of them bit. So, while this soggy clothespin minnow dried, I went back into my father's shop in our basement and tried to make it better.

First, I looked up in the encyclopedia what colors minnows usually were. I found out they were mostly green, black, and white. After my paint dried, I tied my minnow onto my line and gave it a try. Within 20 minutes I caught a beautiful, big bass! Soon I was in business selling clothespin minnows. All the neighborhood kids paid me 25 cents for one of my minnows!

My invention was a success because it was a product people wanted. People, in fact, were anxious to have it. Also, I could easily change my design to make other similar products.

I hope you will become a great inventor. Start by looking around for problems at home, school, or in the environment that you might be able to solve. If you'd like to talk to me about your invention, you can reach me at my E-mail address: stan-mason@snet.net. Best of luck, and happy inventing!

The Mason minnow business

Great Inventors

- 💡 What qualities does someone need to be an inventor?
- 💡 Do inventors need special training?
- 💡 What is the inventive mind?

The Characteristics of an Inventor

You start becoming a great inventor when you start asking questions. Have you ever been curious about something and then began to ask questions in an effort to solve a certain problem? If you have, you're on the road to becoming a great inventor. Inventing is a fun and exciting process. Anyone can become an inventor. You only need to have some natural curiosity, creativity, and inventiveness.

The greatest inventors in the world ask a lot of questions. They also work very hard at inventing. They make mistakes, have good luck, have bad luck, and even start over from the beginning before they finally create a successful invention. Hanging over every inventor's door should be a sign that reads "Practice makes perfect."

Many famous inventors have had their ideas criticized and even rejected. So, inventors need to be confident in themselves and in the worth of their invention. They need to be persistent and not give up their dream. (And, they should keep open minds about the inventions of others!) Here is what some people said about inventions that were once new and groundbreaking. Do you agree with them?

"Heavier-than-air flying machines are impossible."
 —*Lord Kelvin, president, Royal Society, 1895, about the invention of the airplane*

"Everything that can be invented has been invented."
 —*Charles H. Duell, commissioner, U.S. Office of Patents, 1899*

"640 k ought to be enough for anybody."
 —*William Gates, founder, Microsoft Corp., 1981*

What Makes a Great Inventor?

Now, let's find out if you have what it takes to become a great inventor. Get out a piece of paper and a pencil to write down your answers to the Young Inventor's Questionnaire below. You'll discover the traits that you already share with inventors who are successful. There are no wrong or right answers.

The Young Inventor's Questionnaire

1. Do you like to try new things?

2. Do you accept that sometimes you make mistakes?

3. Do you like to build things?

4. Are you curious?

5. Do you work on a task until it is done?

6. Do you like to think of new ways to do things?

7. Do you like to complete puzzles and play games?

8. Do you like to keep notes and make records?

9. Do you like to research things?

10. Do you draw, sketch, or make designs?

11. Are you persistent, which means you don't give up?

Look at all of your "yes" answers. These are the "great inventor" characteristics you already possess!

Try This!

IF YOU WERE GOING TO WRITE A "HELP WANTED" AD FOR AN INVENTOR, WHAT WOULD IT SAY?
WHAT ARE THE MOST IMPORTANT QUALITIES YOU WOULD WANT THAT INVENTOR TO HAVE?

What Is an Invention?

An *invention* is a new device or process. Most inventions are attempts to simplify an existing process. This usually means doing more work in the same or less amount of time. Inventions come about in many ways. Some of the best inventions are very simple, like coat hangers, sewing needles, or paper clips. Other great inventions, like computers, televisions, and spaceships, are complicated and have many parts. Not all inventions, however, are objects. Some are new technologies or processes that will help us in the future.

When people make an existing invention even better, they create an *innovation*. An innovation is an addition or improvement to an existing product or process. Innovations are just as important as inventions. No idea for an innovation is silly. Almost anything that exists can be made better.

Check It Out!

THROUGHOUT HISTORY, HUMANS HAVE BEEN INVENTORS. TODAY'S COMMUNICATIONS INDUSTRY STARTED A LONG TIME AGO WHEN THE FIRST HUMANS DREW PICTURES ON CAVE WALLS. IN 1300 B.C. THE FIRST ALPHABET WAS CREATED, AND THEN IN 1515 A.D. THE FIRST PENCIL WAS INVENTED. IN 1837, SAMUEL F. MORSE DEVELOPED THE TELEGRAPH, AND IN 1867, C. L. SHOLES INVENTED THE TYPEWRITER. MANY YEARS LATER, IN 1942, BERRY ATANASOFF CREATED THE ELECTRONIC COMPUTER. TODAY, INVENTORS ARE CREATING MICROCHIPS, PROCESSORS, PAGERS, MICROWAVE STATIONS, SATELLITES, AND OTHER COMMUNICATION DEVICES TO MAKE OUR LIVES BETTER.

Famous Inventions and Their Inventors

There are thousands of inventions in our world today. Some, like the electric lightbulb and the telephone, are famous as the first modern inventions. Their inventors—Thomas Edison and Alexander Graham Bell—are household names. But there are many other inventions you use every day whose inventors you probably haven't heard of.

On a separate piece of paper, try to match the inventions listed on page 12 with their inventors. An asterisk (*) denotes inventions that are featured in the National Inventors Hall of Fame in Akron, Ohio, which celebrates America's greatest inventions and inventors. Answers are listed at the bottom of page 12.

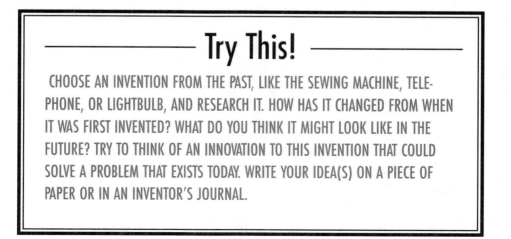

——— Try This! ———

CHOOSE AN INVENTION FROM THE PAST, LIKE THE SEWING MACHINE, TELEPHONE, OR LIGHTBULB, AND RESEARCH IT. HOW HAS IT CHANGED FROM WHEN IT WAS FIRST INVENTED? WHAT DO YOU THINK IT MIGHT LOOK LIKE IN THE FUTURE? TRY TO THINK OF AN INNOVATION TO THIS INVENTION THAT COULD SOLVE A PROBLEM THAT EXISTS TODAY. WRITE YOUR IDEA(S) ON A PIECE OF PAPER OR IN AN INVENTOR'S JOURNAL.

Invention Matchup

INVENTIONS

1. *BULLET-RESISTANT VEST

2. *VARIETY OF PEACHES

3. *PEANUTS AND SWEET POTATOES

4. *XEROX MACHINE

5. *LIQUID ROCKET FUEL

6. ELECTRIC BATTERY

7. *VULCANIZED RUBBER

8. *ANTIFUNGAL ANTIBIOTICS

9. *LASER

10. *RADIO

11. *TEFLON

12. *COMPUTER TECHNOLOGY

13. CORN FLAKES

14. *LEUKEMIA-FIGHTING DRUGS

15. *CORTISONE

INVENTORS

a. PERCY JULIAN

b. LUTHER BURBANK

c. STEPHANIE KWOLEK

d. THEODORE MAIMAN

e. ELIZABETH HAZEN AND RACHEL BROWN

f. ROBERT GODDARD

g. ALESSANDRO VOLTA

h. AN WANG

i. ROY PLUNKETT

j. GUGLIELMO MARCONI

k. JOHN KELLOG

l. GEORGE WASHINGTON CARVER

m. GERTRUDE B. ELION

n. CHARLES GOODYEAR

o. CHESTER CARLSON

[**Answers:** 1. c 2. b 3. l 4. o 5. f 6. g 7. n 8. e 9. d 10. j 11. i 12. h 13. k 14. m 15. a]

Inventors Are Not Scaredy-Cats

by "Curious George" Margolin

WHAT IS AN *INVENTOR*? AN INVENTOR IS ANYONE WHO LIVES IN A WORLD OF POSSIBILITIES AND MAKE-BELIEVE. HE OR SHE IS A PERSON WITH A CURIOUS MIND, AND ONE WHO ALWAYS EXPLORES THE WORLD AROUND HIM OR HER.

AN INVENTOR ASKS WHAT MAKES THINGS WORK, WHY THINGS ARE THE WAY THEY ARE, AND WHY THEY DO THE THINGS THEY DO. HE OR SHE SOLVES PROBLEMS, CREATING SOLUTIONS IN THE FORM OF INVENTIONS THAT OTHER PEOPLE NEVER EVEN CONSIDER.

INVENTORS ARE NOT AFRAID TO MAKE MISTAKES BECAUSE THEY KNOW THEY ARE DOING SOMETHING NEW, DIFFICULT, OR GROUNDBREAKING. THEY ARE MORE CONCERNED WITH DOING SOMETHING IMPORTANT OR WORTHWHILE THAN WITH MAKING A MISTAKE.

IF YOU HAVE CURIOSITY AND CREATIVITY, YOU, TOO, CAN BE A GREAT INVENTOR.

DR. MARGOLIN HAS MORE THAN TWO DOZEN PATENTS, INCLUDING A MOTION PICTURE BACKGROUND SYSTEM USED IN THE FILM 2001: A SPACE ODYSSEY *AND IN SEVERAL JAMES BOND FILMS.*

Women and Minority Inventors

Throughout America's history, scores of women and minority inventors have contributed to making this nation great. Although you don't often hear about them, these famous researchers have experimented with everything from Scotchgard and windshield wipers to coffee and nuclear fission.

Women Inventors

Hattie Alexander developed the cure for *meningitis* during the 1930s. Meningitis is a serious bacterial disease that affects parts of the brain.

Mary Anderson patented windshield wipers in 1903. (To learn more about patents, check out chapter 10.)

Katharine Blodgett, the first woman scientist hired by General Electric's Research Laboratory, discovered how molecules interact. She then used this information to create a nonglare/nonreflective glass.

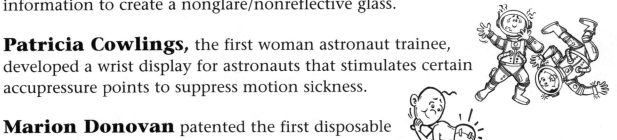

Patricia Cowlings, the first woman astronaut trainee, developed a wrist display for astronauts that stimulates certain accupressure points to suppress motion sickness.

Marion Donovan patented the first disposable diaper in 1951.

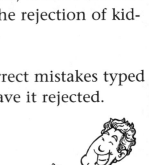

Gertrude B. Elion, the 1988 Nobel Laureate in medicine, created the first two drugs to successfully treat leukemia, a drug to prevent the rejection of kidney transplants, and the first antiviral drug against herpes.

Bette Nesmith Graham invented Liquid Paper to correct mistakes typed on paper. She first introduced her product to IBM only to have it rejected. Years later, her company sold for millions of dollars.

Ruth Handler created the Barbie doll in 1956.

Stephanie Kwolek created Kevlar, a synthetic fiber strong enough to stop bullets. Kevlar is the material used to make bullet-proof vests.

Patsy Sherman spilled some latex mixture on a tennis shoe and invented one of the 10 textile miracles of the modern world: Scotchgard.

A Celebration of Women

IN 1990, THE U.S. PATENT OFFICE CELEBRATED ITS 200TH ANNIVERSARY WITH A SPECIAL EXHIBIT ON WOMEN INVENTORS, TITLED "WOMAN'S PLACE IS IN THE PATENT OFFICE." PROFESSOR FRED AMRAM OF THE UNIVERSITY OF MINNESOTA DISPLAYED OLD INVENTIONS THAT SHOWED THE ACCOMPLISHMENTS OF WOMEN INVENTORS.

Minority Inventors

Eric Adolphe developed a wrist device and laptop computer that allows law enforcement officials to detect and track convicted drunk drivers who are driving even though their licenses have been suspended.

Luis Alvarez was a famous Hispanic scientist who developed a radar beam so narrow it could guide an aircraft through fog. In 1968, Dr. Alvarez won the Nobel Prize for his invention of the hydrogen bubble chamber, an instrument of great power and precision.

George Washington Carver, one of the most famous African American inventors, developed crops of peanuts, sweet potatoes, pecans, and soybeans. His inventions in the late 1800s and early 1900s freed Southern farmers from their reliance on cotton as a crop. However, Carver lived too long ago to have his valuable work officially recognized. It wasn't until 1930 that the U.S. Patent and Trademark Office approved patents for new forms of plants.

Charles Drew created the first blood plasma bank. He also was one of the first African American inventors to be featured on a U.S. postage stamp.

Garrett Morgan invented the traffic light and the gas mask. He wore his mask while rescuing workers trapped in a tunnel in Ohio.

Madam C. J. Walker invented over 14 different hair products for women in 1905. At the time, her manufacturing company was the largest African American–owned company in the United States.

The Invention of Braille

IN 1824, A 15-YEAR-OLD BOY NAMED LOUIS BRAILLE GAVE BLIND PEOPLE THE KEY TO INDEPENDENCE. USING A SYSTEM OF RAISED DOT PATTERNS ON PAPER THAT REPRESENTED LETTERS AND WORDS, HE CREATED A NEW SYSTEM OF READING. TODAY WE CALL THE SYSTEM BRAILLE AFTER ITS INVENTOR, AND THE FAMOUS CLINICS THROUGH AMERICA THAT TEACH THE BLIND ARE NAMED BRAILLE INSTITUTES.

MEET A SUPERSTAR INVENTOR . . .

Joshua Gonzales
Age: 12
Home: Santa Ana, California
Invention Name: Toy Track
Invention Category: Toy/Medical

The Problem: Joshua, a disabled student, observed that his friends in the severely handicapped class at school had a hard time keeping their toy cars on their stander trays when they were playing with them. A teacher or peer would pick them up, but the students would only knock them off again.

Joshua's Answer: Joshua and his teacher brainstormed ideas to solve the problem. They tried out several of their ideas. First, they put the cars in a shallow box on a student's tray. This didn't work because it was too hard for the students to play with the cars while reaching over the sides of the box. Next, Joshua tied a string to one end of the car. He then tied the other end of the string to the tray. This didn't work because the students still knocked the car off the tray—instead of hitting the floor, the car dangled from the string. Joshua and the teacher then tried the Toy Track idea.

They pulled the string through openings in the toy car, and then, using duct tape, they secured both ends of the string to the bottom of the tray. The students could then play with the car along the string, using a hand-over-hand technique. The car could not fall off the tray, because it was secured by the taped-down string on both sides of the tray.

While testing his invention, Joshua used different types of string and, instead of cars, balls. He found that yarn broke too easily when the students pulled on it. Kite string was too "slippery" and difficult for the students to handle. Packing string worked the best! He also discovered that a tennis ball substituted best for a car on the track. It could move sideways and also bounce.

According to Joshua, the best parts of creating his invention were showing the other students how to use the hand-over-hand technique and giving an oral report about the invention to his mainstream science class.

——— What a Great Idea! ———

WHAT IDEAS CAN YOU COME UP WITH THAT WOULD HELP SOMEONE WHO IS DISABLED? HERE ARE A FEW TO KEEP IN MIND.

- A DEVICE FOR HARD-OF-HEARING PERSONS
- A PROSTHESIS TO HELP SOMEONE WALK
- AN INSTRUMENT FOR HANDICAPPED PEOPLE WHO CAN'T STAND UP
- A WALKING CANE FOR DISABLED PEOPLE THAT LIGHTS UP OR GLOWS IN THE DARK

Getting Started

- What steps does an inventor go through to create an invention?
- Is inventing a random process?
- What is an invention fair?

What Is an Invention Fair Project?

An *invention fair project* is a product or process that has been newly created and entered into a contest known as a fair. Invention fairs are very similar to science fairs. Judges rate the inventions and then present awards to the projects they feel are the most practical, unique, and creative. Invention fairs are usually held from January to May and can be school, district, state, or even national contests. Often the young inventor who wins at his or her school fair goes on to a district fair and then perhaps to a state fair. The best inventions can go on to national competitions and win a variety of awards. The judges at these fairs are real-life scientists and inventors. (The judging criteria will be discussed later in this book.)

An invention fair project can be an invention or an innovation. Do you remember the difference between the two? (They were discussed in chapter 1.) In case you don't, here is a reminder: An invention is something that is totally new. An innovation makes a current product or process better. Which type of project you create for your fair will probably depend on the problem you choose to solve. As you research possible solutions to your problem, you will discover whether an invention or an innovation would make the best solution. In either case, you will use the steps in the invention process to design, build, and test your creation.

A great invention takes time. It is not simply a poster display of pictures cut from magazines, an Internet printout, or words copied from an encyclopedia or textbook. In fact, those things are just presentations of other people's work. Your invention fair project will be your own original work. It will show the problem you uncovered and how you found the solution through research, experimentation, and trial and error. It will show how you gathered your materials, as well as designed, built, and tested your creation.

Along the way, you will seek help from teachers, parents, adult friends, and business people or inventors you may know. You'll be putting a lot of work into creating something that will help your family, pets, plants, even people who are handicapped or have disabilities. Remember, great inventions can come from the simplest or the craziest ideas.

The Seven Steps to Inventing

When completing science fair projects, people use the scientific method as a guide for conducting experiments and testing theories. When creating your invention fair project, you will follow the seven steps of the invention process. Unlike the scientific method, the invention process may vary from one invention to another. For example, if an inventor comes up with his or her idea during research (and not before), steps 1 and 2 may follow step 4. The order of the steps outlined below are the most common, especially for young inventors.

Step 1: Look around to find a problem you want to solve. Do you hate how your desk at school never stays open? Do you feel sorry for the birds unable to get seed out of your backyard bird feeder? All sorts of inventions—for your school, your home—are just waiting to be created.

Step 2: Start an inventor's journal. You will write everything about your invention in this notebook. If you already have some ideas, get a bound book, like a composition book, for your journal as soon as possible. (See chapter 3 for details.) Your journal is the documentation that proves what you are inventing is your own idea. You'll want to write down each step of the invention process.

Step 3: Brainstorm solutions to the problem. This means anything goes! No idea is too crazy or dumb. Write every single one down in your journal. Then pick three or four of your best to investigate further.

Step 4: Do some research. Find out if your ideas for solutions have already been invented. If so, head back to step 1. Otherwise, narrow your choices to the single best idea and proceed.

Step 5: Draw some sketches of what your invention could look like. Then make a list of everything you would need to build it.

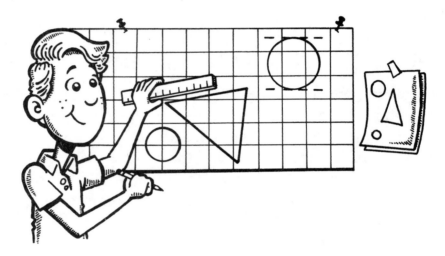

Step 6: Gather materials—what you'll need to build the breadboard, which is the first model of your invention. (See chapter 8.) You will probably need a parent, teacher, or other adult to help you.

Step 7: Build it! Then test your invention to see if it works. Can you make it even better? Make as many adjustments as you think might be needed.

Here's a great idea that shows how one superstar inventor followed the steps to solve a problem he discovered right in his neighbor's backyard.

MEET A SUPERSTAR INVENTOR . . .

Doug Krailo
Age: 10
Home: Nashua, New Hampshire
Invention Name: The LITTERally
FUN RAFT, Incorporated
Invention Category: Recreation/Toys

The Problem: "Each summer I needed to buy at least one new raft to use in our neighbor's swimming pool. No matter how much money I spent, or how durable and sturdy the raft seemed to be, it would deflate or get a hole either before the end of the summer or by the beginning of the next summer."

Doug's Answer: "I looked around for a material that would hold up in the pool after a lot of hard use. I learned that in order for something to float, it has to be filled with air. I thought about plastic bottles. I noticed that people often throw plastic bottles on the ground rather than recycling or placing them in a garbage can. If I could make my raft out of bottles I found on the ground, I could help solve that problem, too.

"I tested a few plastic bottles in the bathtub. With the caps screwed on tightly, they floated. Now I needed a way to hold the bottles together. I learned how to sew on a sewing machine and sewed two large pieces of colored cotton material together. The material held the bottles OK. My mom put in a zipper for me because

I wanted to be able to open the raft and replace any bottles that got crushed. After measuring the diameter of the plastic bottles, I decided to divide the cloth into five equal pockets. Each pocket would hold five bottles.

"I collected enough bottles to fill the pockets and then tested the raft. It floated when I put it in my neighbor's pool. Then I climbed on, and it held me, too. I tested it with my dad. It held him also. The raft lasted all summer without me having to replace even one bottle."

What a Great Idea!

HERE ARE SOME MORE INTERESTING AND UNUSUAL IDEAS FOR SPORT ITEMS OR TOYS YOU MIGHT WANT TO TRY INVENTING.

- A TRAMPOLINE WITH ADJUSTABLE TENSIONS
- NEW SNOW BOOTS FOR KIDS THAT KEEP FEET *REALLY* WARM
- A PAIR OF WATER SKIS THAT MAKE IT EASY FOR KIDS TO DO TRICKS
- SOFT TOYS FOR BABIES

Choosing a Great Idea

Deciding what to choose for your project can be the most challenging part. Look around you. Think about a problem you encounter in your life. Great ideas are everywhere! Maybe you've had trouble fastening your seat belt, cleaning your room quickly enough, or feeding your pet regularly. Do some research to learn more about the thing that's troubling you or how people have already tried to improve it. You may end up designing an entire invention project around this one thing. Here are some tips to start you on your search.

Read stories about famous inventions and inventors. Ask the reference librarian for help locating information in magazines and journals. Surf the Internet on an educational search engine or encyclopedia site. Ask your teachers to order videotapes on special topics. Watch educational television shows on PBS stations or the Discovery Channel.

Look around your home, school, neighborhood, and community. Then ask yourself these questions:

Are there problems your family and friends have that you could solve?

Can you help solve problems for people with special needs, such as the disabled?

Have you uncovered problems of the poor and disadvantaged that you might be able to solve?

Do you find problems with pets in your area?

? Are there ways to help preserve the environment or endangered animal species?

? Could you create alternative energy sources or more effective recycling programs?

? Are there things to improve around your house or parents' offices?

? Could you create a new entertainment activity or toy?

Write down all the ideas that occur to you. You'll be surprised at all the possibilities that come to mind.

Once you have narrowed down your invention project choices, interview an adult who works in a job related to your idea.
Contact a working inventor through your local inventor's group. You'll find such telephone numbers in the yellow pages of the telephone book. You might also want to talk with a scientist who is an expert in your area. Call your local college or university, or write to the Science Center, University of Missouri, PO Box 838, Columbia, MO 65205, or call (313) 882-2914 to find out how to get in touch with the appropriate person. Your science, math, industrial arts, or technology teacher is another good source for invention project ideas. Talking to these experts will not only help you pick the best invention idea but will also assist you in your creation process.

After you choose the idea you think will be the most fun and exciting, ask yourself the following questions: Is my idea unique? Needed? Useful? Is it safe as well as helpful to many people? Is it marketable? Would people buy it? If you answered "yes" to these questions, you may just have a great invention project idea!

Evaluating Your Idea

In your inventor's journal, make a chart like the one below to evaluate whether your idea will be a great invention fair project. The "Needs Improvement" and "What I Can Do to Make It Better" sections will help you improve your project so it will be a winning entry.

Evaluation of My Project

My project is an: _____ Invention   _____ Innovation

My category is_____

PROJECT CHARACTERISTICS	YES / NO (CHECK IF "YES"/ X IF "NO")	NEEDS IMPROVEMENT (CHECK IF "YES")	WHAT I CAN DO TO MAKE IT BETTER
ORIGINAL			
CREATIVE			
SIMPLE			
INEXPENSIVE			
STURDY			
ENVIRONMENTALLY SAFE			
CLEVERLY NAMED			
VALUABLE TO MANY PEOPLE			

Open Your Mind to Possibilities

by Dr. Gary Nelson, President, Edison's Inventors Association

ON A PRETTY AUGUST DAY, OLE EVINRUDE WAS ROWING HIS BOAT TO HIS FAVORITE ISLAND PICNIC SPOT. AS HE ROWED, HE WATCHED HIS ICE CREAM MELT AND WISHED HE HAD A FASTER WAY TO GET TO THE ISLAND. THAT MOMENT INSPIRED HIS INVENTION, THE OUTBOARD MOTOR!

HAVE YOU EVER HAD AN IDEA TO IMPROVE A PRODUCT? HOW MANY TIMES HAVE YOU SAID, "I WISH SOMEONE WOULD MAKE A _____ "(FILL IN THE BLANK YOURSELF). THE NEXT TIME THIS HAPPENS TO YOU, SIT DOWN, RELAX, AND LET YOUR IMAGINATION RUN WITH IT. GET YOUR THOUGHTS TOGETHER, AND BEGIN TO DEVELOP IDEAS. IDEAS ARE USELESS UNLESS THEY ARE NURTURED. ONLY THEN CAN THEY GROW INTO INVENTIONS. AND INVENTIONS CAN CHANGE THE COURSE OF HISTORY! KEEP YOUR MIND OPEN TO POSSIBILITIES. YOU WILL PROBABLY DISCOVER THAT YOUR IDEAS ARE NOT AS SILLY AS YOU THOUGHT. REMEMBER THAT EVERYONE HAS THE ABILITY TO BE CREATIVE AND TO APPLY HIM- OR HERSELF. THIS IS WHAT INVENTING IS ALL ABOUT.

Invention Categories

There are thousands of problems that haven't been solved, and the United States Patent and Trademark Office (USPTO) puts these problems into 14 categories. A *category* is a broad topic, for example, communication or energy. You may choose one or more categories for your project. These are the 14 categories: medical, energy, home, recreational, food preparation, engineering, transportation, communication, power generation, farming, toys, personal, entertainment, and office. Many school fairs do not use all of these categories. Other fairs add

categories, for example: pets, the disabled, time-savers, safety, and personal improvement.

Once you've picked your best idea, figure out its category. Write your idea and its category in your inventor's journal:

The most important problem I found was _____

_____

_____

_____. It falls

under the _____ category.

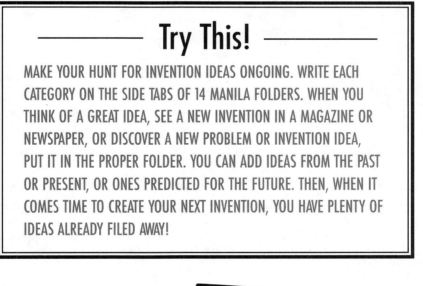

—— Try This! ——

MAKE YOUR HUNT FOR INVENTION IDEAS ONGOING. WRITE EACH CATEGORY ON THE SIDE TABS OF 14 MANILA FOLDERS. WHEN YOU THINK OF A GREAT IDEA, SEE A NEW INVENTION IN A MAGAZINE OR NEWSPAPER, OR DISCOVER A NEW PROBLEM OR INVENTION IDEA, PUT IT IN THE PROPER FOLDER. YOU CAN ADD IDEAS FROM THE PAST OR PRESENT, OR ONES PREDICTED FOR THE FUTURE. THEN, WHEN IT COMES TIME TO CREATE YOUR NEXT INVENTION, YOU HAVE PLENTY OF IDEAS ALREADY FILED AWAY!

MEET A SUPERSTAR INVENTOR . . .

Charlie Matykiewicz
Age: 13
Home: Windermere, Florida
Invention Name: Charlie's Automatic
Dog Washer
Invention Category: Home/Pets

The Problem: "My dog, Candy, was always coming home dirty. I thought it would be great to find a way to wash Candy without getting dirty myself. My dad and I talked about various solutions, and thought I should try to create an automatic dog washer."

Charlie's Answer: "I built a frame using some PVC pipe. The frame had spray nozzles set up all around, which sprayed the dog when she was put inside. To keep her inside, there was a clip that attached to her collar. A belly strap kept her from sitting down. A hose on the bottom of the washer supplied the water. There also was on-off valve. Inside this PVC frame, Candy could get washed while walking around, but she could not break the washer.

"My dad and I tried out my PVC washer at a dog-washing fund-raiser in Jupiter, Florida. I found that some dogs didn't like it, especially pit bulls, but others loved it. Owners started to ask me how much I would charge to sell them one. They said they would pay anywhere between $25 and $40!

"I have won many invention contests and appeared on radio and television shows. A patent attorney even offered to help me patent my invention. This was great because patents can cost up to $5,000. I applied for my patent but did not get it because a few car washers are similar in function and design. I'm working on a new design so that I can apply again. I think it's very important to keep trying."

What a Great Idea!

HERE ARE OTHER IDEAS FOR PET-RELATED INVENTIONS YOU MIGHT WANT TO TRY.

- AN AUTOMATIC CAT FEEDER FOR WHEN OWNERS GO ON VACATION
- A NEW KIND OF AQUARIUM FOR FRESHWATER FISH
- CLOTHING FOR PETS LIVING IN COLD PLACES
- HARD, CHEWABLE TOYS FOR PUPPIES
- A DOG HOUSE THAT EXPANDS TO FIT DOGS AS THEY GROW LARGER

Invention or Innovation?

If, while researching your invention idea, you discover it has already been created, don't give up! You have some *design options*. A design option is a new way of looking at designing or creating something. You can rework a current product or process to make a different, more attractive, or more efficient model. That is, you can make an innovation. For example, pretend you wanted to invent a clothespin and then found out it was already a product. Would you just give up? No! Instead, you would explore your options and invent a new or improved clothespin.

To help figure out how to turn your invention into an innovation, ask yourself these questions:

1. What else can this be used for and how can I change it to meet this need?

2. What material(s) could be substituted in the design?

3. How could the design be modified?

4. How could it be simplified?

5. What if the product were larger or smaller?

6. What else could be added? (Be careful with this one. You don't want to add any unnecessary items. See chapter 6.)

Check It Out!

THERE ARE VERY FEW INVENTIONS THAT DO NOT OWE SOMETHING TO EARLIER INVENTIONS. MOST MODERN INVENTIONS ARE COMBINATIONS OF PIECES, PARTS, AND TECHNOLOGIES CREATED BY OTHER PEOPLE. PUT TOGETHER IN A NEW AND INNOVATIVE WAY, THESE NEW PRODUCTS WORK DIFFERENTLY TO SERVE DIFFERENT PURPOSES. THIS MAKES IT DIFFICULT TO CREDIT ANY ONE INVENTOR WITH HAVING BEEN THE FIRST IN HIS OR HER FIELD TO INVENT SOMETHING.

FOR EXAMPLE, THERE WERE SEVERAL MORE OR LESS SUCCESSFUL DESIGNS FOR STEAMERS THAT WERE BUILT IN THE LATE 1700S. BUT, IN 1807, AMERICAN ROBERT FULTON BUILT HIS *CLERMONT* STEAMBOAT. USING THE TECHNOLOGIES OF THE STEAMERS THAT PRECEDED HIS, HE WAS ABLE TO CREATE THE FIRST PASSENGER- AND FREIGHT-CARRYING STEAMBOAT. WITH A PADDLE WHEEL AND PROPELLER-DRIVEN STEAMER, HIS STEAMBOAT TRAVELED REGULARLY UP THE HUDSON RIVER.

The Inventor's Journal

 What is an inventor's journal?

 How do I make my journal?

 What should I include in it?

 What is a witness?

What Is a Journal?

The inventor's journal, sometimes called the inventor's log, is an organized diary of all your invention ideas. It is the dated record of the steps you take, as well as all the help you receive. Your journal will contain your ideas, research, notes, sketches, drawings, photographs, model tests and test results, descriptions of the parts you used, and all invention-related costs. (All of your drawings should be carefully labeled.)

Your journal is very important. It will serve as proof that you alone thought up the idea for your invention and carried out the steps of the invention process. You can even include a videotape of how your invention works or how you built it. Just remember to have your videotape witnessed by someone else. Read on for information on witnesses.

Types of Journals

There are many ways to make a journal, but most inventors use a writing book. This can be a formal laboratory book purchased at a scientific supply store (you'll find a list on page 65) or one you make yourself using a file folder. You can even use a composition book. Whatever you choose, remember it's best to use a journal with bound pages that are sewn together rather than one with spiral pages that can easily be removed, misplaced, or lost. Your journal should have lined or graph paper and a cover. Its pages should be numbered.

For Younger Inventors

For a younger inventor's journal, a file folder journal works great. You can staple a few pieces of notebook paper into a letter-size manila folder. Write "My Invention" on the cover, and include the following information inside the journal:

My name is . . .
The name of my invention is . . .
My materials are . . .
What I did today:
My inventions works as follows:
My invention looks like . . .
The parts of my invention are . . .
My witnesses are . . .

Don't forget to also include your notes and labeled sketches.

For Older Inventors

Journals for older inventors may be as many as 50 to 100 pages. However, they do not have to be that long. In addition to including the information listed for younger inventors, document the following:

identifying who my invention will help

researching my idea

creating a detailed design

testing the parts

improving and changing the parts

pricing and costs

conducting a patent search

finding manufacturing sources

Witnessing Your Journal

You will write in your journal whenever you have an idea, revise your invention, or purchase a supply. This could be several times a week or even every day. You therefore want to make sure you protect all your great work. You should create special lines or a witness section at the bottom of each page of your journal. This is where a witness will sign and date your journal after you add something new to it. You can choose to have your journal witnessed after each new entry, once a week, or every two weeks. It is up to you. Just be sure to have all your pages witnessed on a regular basis.

A parent, teacher, or other adult can be your witness. He or she will initial or print his or her name and the date on the witness lines at the bottom of the page. Some inventors choose to initial or sign and date the entry along with the witness. These signatures will prove that you alone did all the work and that these are your ideas. Below is a sample journal page with a witness section.

Here's how one young inventor made sure she put each of her five designs in her journal and had them witnessed.

The Younger Inventor's Journal

My invention name: _____

What I did today: _____

_____

_____

Here is a labeled sketch of what I designed today:

This is how it works: _____

_____

_____

My signature (or initials) _____ Date _____

Witness signature (or initials) _____ Date _____

MEET A SUPERSTAR INVENTOR . . .

Grace Reynolds
Age: 11
Home: Tustin, California
Invention Name: Water Polo Ball Holder
Invention Category: Recreation

The Problem: "I play on a water polo team, and whenever my team is scrimmaging or doing drills, balls are always floating in our way. The balls prevent us from doing our drills quickly and smoothly. During warm-ups at tournaments, we sometimes lose balls because the ones not being used float to other parts of the pool where other teams are warming up. They get mixed in with these other teams' balls, and they end up taking them home."

Grace's Answer: "I wanted to find a way to keep our unused balls from floating all over the pool. I decided to make a ring to hold the balls together. First, I sketched out what I wanted the ring to look like. Next, I decided to test out my drawing by making a model. I took two hula hoops that I had in my garage, along with two water noodles from my grandparents' pool. My mom took me to the hardware store to buy two acrylic sheets. They cost seven dollars total. I then found a hand drill, duct tape, and a little wire from my garage. I thought I could use these tools to put my parts together.

"First, I used just one hula hoop with a noodle around it. When I tested it in the pool and tried to throw balls into it, the balls just popped out. The ring was not tall enough. I then tried other versions, adding the acrylic sheets to the ring. My grandpa helped me make the holes in the acrylic sheets with a hand drill, and I wired them onto the hoop. This did not work either because the ring fell back when the balls hit the sheets.

"Finally, I decided to add an extra hoop on top of the acrylic sheets. When I tested this last design in the pool, it worked. I then tested it at a tournament in San Diego, and all the players loved it. So did the coaches.

"In total, I made five models and noted everything in my journal. I drew sketches of the five different models. I wrote why they did not work and how the final water polo ball holder was made. Everyone signed my journal: my mom, grandma, grandpa, and coach."

What a Great Idea

HERE ARE SOME MORE INVENTION IDEAS. THEY HAVE TO DO WITH SPORTS AND RECREATION.

- A HOLDER OR CASE FOR TENNIS BALLS AND RACKETS
- A RACK FOR KEEPING BICYCLES PARKED OUTSIDE
- A DEVICE TO HOLD SPORTS EQUIPMENT ON WHEELCHAIRS OR WALKERS
- A NEW TYPE OF PLAYGROUND EQUIPMENT
- A NEW SPORT WITH RULES AND INSTRUCTIONS

Check It Out!

MECHANIC AND INVENTOR DANIEL DRAWBAUGH WAS VERY SORRY HE DIDN'T KEEP A WITNESSED JOURNAL WHEN HE INVENTED HIS VERY SIMPLE TELEPHONE. EVEN THOUGH MANY PEOPLE COULD TESTIFY THAT HE HAD TALKED OVER THIS CRUDE TELEPHONE-LIKE DEVICE LONG BEFORE ALEXANDER GRAHAM BELL FILED A PATENT APPLICATION, DRAWBAUGH COULD NOT GET HIS PHONE PATENTED.

IN 1888, THE SUPREME COURT OF THE UNITED STATES REJECTED HIS PATENT CLAIM. THE VERBAL TESTIMONY OF WITNESSES DID HIM NO GOOD. WITHOUT WRITTEN, DATED PROOF THAT HAS BEEN SIGNED BY WITNESSES, A PATENT WILL NOT BE GRANTED BY THE U.S. PATENT OFFICE. AS A RESULT, ALEXANDER GRAHAM BELL BECAME FAMOUS, WEALTHY, AND RENOWNED AS ONE OF THE GREATEST INVENTORS OF ALL TIME.

THIS WAS NOT THE ONLY TIME AN INVENTOR FAILED TO GET CREDIT FOR HIS OR HER INVENTION BECAUSE OF NOT RECORDING THE EVIDENCE. THE CLAIMS OF THE INVENTORS OF THE CAR, COMPUTER, AND LASER WERE ALL DISPUTED.

Here is a quick checklist to help you remember how to keep a proper inventor's journal.

Do . . . ✔

- write in permanent black ink.
- draw a line through any error.
- use a bound notebook.
- date your notes in chronological order.
- include sketches, photos, and/or videos.
- include labels for all picture parts.
- sign and date all entries.
- pick one name for your invention and always use it.

Don't . . . ✗

- use pencil.
- use correction fluid or erasers.
- use a spiral or three-ringed notebook.
- skip around.
- sketch on loose pieces of paper.
- include a picture without labeling it.
- forget to have entries witnessed.
- call your invention different names.

Planning Your Project

CHAPTER 4

- How long will it take to create my invention?
- What things should I plan on doing each week?
- How do I create my own project timeline?

A Project Timeline

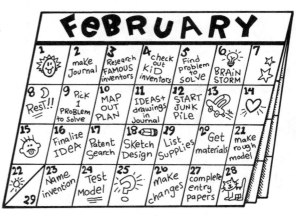

So, you've figured out what problem you are going to solve with your invention. Great! Now it is time to start thinking about how to best solve that problem, ideally within a reasonable amount of time. Good inventors always make a plan. Before they begin their project, they figure out how much time each step in their invention process will take.

Below is a six-week plan, or *timeline,* based on those of many young inventors. It should take at least six weeks to get your ideas together, do your research, create your designs, conduct your experiments, build, test, and make changes to your project before you get it just right. This is a proven guide for young inventors, and it should help you as you plot the course of your own invention.

Of course, if you need more time than is allotted here to complete any aspect of your invention, add time to your own personal plan. Remember, inventors work at different speeds and get bursts of creativity and energy at different times. Some make more changes and revisions than others do. But most inventors know what to expect of themselves. This way, they can estimate how long their creation will take.

Most importantly, if you are a first-time inventor, take your time and do a good job. It is the final product that counts. However, try to finish within a reasonable amount of time, especially if you have only a month or two before the invention fair.

The Six-Week Plan

Week 1

Create your inventor's journal.

Research famous inventions and inventors.

Learn about other kid inventors.

Identify problems that need solving.

Brainstorm ways to solve those problems, writing all your ideas down in your journal.

Week 2

Pick one problem to solve, and think about how to solve it.

Map out your personal six-week plan. Adjust time periods, if needed.

Enter your ideas and drawings in your journal.

Start to gather inexpensive and recyclable materials.
(These will come in handy when you begin to build your model.)*

Week 3

Decide on the best way to solve your problem. That is, finalize your invention idea.

Complete a patent search to find out if your invention has already been made.

Sketch your design, and label your drawing.

List supplies you need (with prices) in your journal.

* Will be discussed later in this book.

Gather those materials.

Make your first, rough model (breadboard) to prove your invention works.*

Week 4

Name your invention.

Test your breadboard model.

Change any features (redesign) to make it work better.

Complete the entry papers for the invention fair.*

Week 5

Ask others what they think about your idea and your model.

Using that feedback, make more changes to improve your invention.

Think of a clever slogan or jingle for the title on your display board.

Create the display board for your invention.*

Week 6

Get ready for the invention fair.

Put finishing touches on your display board.

Put finishing touches on your invention model.

Practice your oral presentation.*

* Will be discussed later in this book.

Questions and Investigation

by Dr. LaMoine Motz
Coordinator, Science Education, Oakland County Schools, and Past President, National Science Teachers Association (NSTA)

EXPERIENCE THE WORLD AROUND YOU, EXCHANGE INFORMATION ABOUT WHAT YOU SEE, AND YOU MAY JUST INVENT SOMETHING THAT WILL HELP NOT ONLY YOU BUT ALSO MANY, MANY OTHERS.

THE KEY TO DISCOVERING AND UNDERSTANDING THE SCIENCE AND TECHNOLOGY AROUND US IS ASKING QUESTIONS. ASKING QUESTIONS ENABLES YOU TO UNCOVER THE MANY UNKNOWN WORLDS AROUND YOU. THOUGH YOU WILL NOT BE ABLE TO FIND ANSWERS TO ALL YOUR QUESTIONS, YOU WILL LEARN A LOT OF WONDERFUL AND INSPIRING INFORMATION.

SHARE YOUR IDEAS WITH YOUR PARENTS AND TEACHERS. TELL THEM ABOUT SOMETHING YOU WOULD LIKE TO INVENT, A CREATION THAT WOULD HELP SOMEONE DO SOMETHING BETTER OR THAT WOULD HELP YOU DO SOMETHING MORE EASILY OR QUICKLY. LISTEN TO ANY ADVICE THEY MAY GIVE. USE RESOURCES SUCH AS THE LIBRARY, ENCYCLOPEDIAS, THE INTERNET, OR EVEN PEOPLF IN YOUR COMMUNITY TO FIND ANSWERS TO ANY QUESTIONS YOU MAY HAVE. THEN BEGIN TO CREATE YOUR INVENTION.

REMEMBER, INVENTING INVOLVES TRIAL AND ERROR—TRYING, FAILING, AND THEN TRYING AGAIN. SO, YOU NEED TO BE PATIENT. YOUR CONCLU- SIONS MAY NEED TO BE MODIFIED AS YOU MAKE NEW DISCOVERIES. THAT'S OK. THIS PROCESS WILL HELP YOU THINK MORE CLEARLY AND CRITICALLY AND GAIN CONFIDENCE IN YOUR ABILITY TO SOLVE PROBLEMS AND MAKE YOUR INVENTION.

Research and Resources

- What is research?
- Where can I go to research my invention?
- What is the difference between primary and secondary research?

What Is Research?

Research is the method by which you gather information, also called *data*. You can find information almost anywhere: from teachers, other inventors, and professionals; at libraries; on the Internet; and from inventing organizations. You can conduct your own experiments and surveys, interview experts, or observe intriguing occurrences. Research can help you find data that will help you better understand your topic. It can provide you with interesting details you may not have thought of before. It can

even give you new ideas about changing a part of or adding a feature to your invention.

You should conduct research while searching for your invention idea, as well as after you've picked your problem to solve. Remember that step 3 in the six-week plan is to discover whether or not your idea has been created by someone else. This will determine whether your project is an invention or an innovation or whether you need to rework your design so that it is different from an existing project. Look back at page 30 to review what to do when your invention idea turns out to be an innovation.

Primary vs. Secondary Research

There are two different kinds of research that you will conduct: *primary research* and *secondary research*. You should record both kinds in your inventor's journal.

Primary Research

When you obtain information by observing something directly or performing your own experiment or survey, the information you gather is called primary research. Primary research is *only* information you gather yourself.

Secondary Research

Information you find in libraries, books, magazines, and newspapers; on television; or from movie documentaries or the Internet is called secondary research. This is research or information that has already been studied, published, or filmed by someone else.

Interviews with experts may be primary or secondary research, depending on the information that person gives you. If, for example, someone relates to you the details of an event that he or she observed, the information is secondary. On the other hand, if someone shows you how he or she sets up a laboratory so you can get ideas about how to create your own, that information is primary. If you have questions about primary and secondary research while conducting your research, ask a parent or teacher for help.

MEET A SUPERSTAR INVENTOR . . .

Allison Sacco
Age: 11
Home: Barrington, Rhode Island
Invention Name: The Invisible IV
Invention Category: Medical

The Problem: "When I was little, I was in the hospital a lot. I often thought about how hard the hospital was for me. I hated IVs almost as much as surgery, and I realized that many other kids feel the same way. I wanted to find a way to make the dreaded IV just a little easier to bear."

Allison's Answer: "I thought a cover over the IV needle might make a kid forget about the IV. So, I began to do research on this subject. Through trial and error, I started to plan my invention.

"First, I drew several designs. Next I experimented with materials. I thought squares might work well. But it was difficult to figure out how to adjust the square for different wrist and arm sizes. The cover also had to allow the child to move his or her hand. I thought of using Velcro straps to help with this problem. I placed the 2-inch-long strips widthwise to adjust the jacket (the IV cover) for wrist size. They work like the Velcro straps on tennis shoes—they can be looser or tighter as needed. I made sure every material was safe to protect from choking, dangerous chemicals, or irritants, and that it was washable, and soft for comfort."

What a Great Idea!

HERE ARE SOME MORE INTERESTING AND UNUSUAL IDEAS FOR HEALTH AND MEDICAL DEVICES YOU MIGHT WANT TO TRY INVENTING.

- A SPECIAL HOSPITAL BED FOR KIDS THAT ALLOWS THEM TO COLOR, DO HOMEWORK, AND PLAY
- A SPECIAL ANTISEPTIC CREAM THAT TURNS COLORS WHEN THE WOUND IS HEALED
- A NEW CHILDREN'S MEDICAL ALERT DEVICE
- A NEW TYPE OF EXAMINATION TABLE FOR KIDS IN THE DOCTOR'S OFFICE

Books and Magazines

You can find a huge supply of information about inventors and inventions in books, magazines, and newspapers. The following list is just a small sample of books and magazines you might be able to use for your project. Remember to list in your inventor's journal all the materials you read. From your notes, you will make your own *bibliography* for your project. A bibliography is an alphabetical list of resources. It should include all the books, magazines, newspaper articles, encyclopedias, and any other primary and secondary resources you  use. Alphabetize your bibliography by the author's last name. Also include the title of the book, location of the publisher, name of the publisher, copyright date, and pages you read. When listing interviews or discussions with experts, write down the name of the person, the date and time of your conversation, the location (if applicable), and what you discussed.

Here is a list of books you may find helpful.

Aaseng, Nathan. *The Problem Solvers: People Who Turned Problems into Products*. Minneapolis, Minn.: Lerner Publications, 1989.

Ardley, Neil. *How Things Work: 100 Ways Parents and Kids Can Share the Secret of Technology*. New York: Reader's Digest Association, 1995.

Caney, Stephen. *Invention Book*. New York: Workman Publishing, 1985.

Clements, Gillian. *The Picture History of Great Inventions*. New York: Alfred A. Knopf, 1994.

Davies, Eryl. *Inventions*. Boston, Mass.: DK Publishing, 1995.

Diagram Group Staff. *Historical Inventions on File*. New York: Facts on File, 1994.

Editors of World Book. *Inventors and Inventions: A Supplement to Childcraft—The How & Why Library*. Chicago, Ill.: World Book, 1993.

Gates, Phil. *Nature Got There First: Inventions Inspired by Nature*. Chatham, N.J.: Kingfisher Books, 1995.

Harris, Tina, et al. *Inventions and Discoveries*. Carson, Calif.: Educational Insights, 1989.

Haskins, Jim. *Outward Dreams: Black Inventors and Their Inventions*. New York: Walker and Company, 1992.

Jones, Charlotte F. *Mistakes That Worked*. New York: Doubleday, 1994.

Lawson, Robert. *Ben and Me*. New York: Little, Brown & Co., 1939.

MacDonald, Anne L. *Feminine Ingenuity: How Women Inventors Changed America*. New York: Ballantine Books, 1994.

Noonan, Jeoffrey J. *Nineteenth Century Inventors*. New York: Facts on File, 1992.

Pollard, Michael. *The Light Bulb and How It Changed the World*. New York: Facts on File, 1995.

The Rejects: People and Products That Outsmarted the Experts. Minneapolis, Minn.: Lerner Publications, 1989.

Showell, Ellen H., and Fred M. B. Amram. *From Indian Corn to Outer Space: Women Invent in America*. Peterborough, N.H. Coblestone Publishing, 1995.

Taylor, Barbara. *Be an Inventor*. San Diego, Calif.: Harcourt Brace, 1987.

Turvey, Peter. *Inventions: Inventors and Ingenious Ideas*. Danbury, Conn.: Franklin Watts, 1994.

Twentieth Century Inventors. New York: Facts on File, 1991.

Vare, Ethlie Ann, and Greg Ptacek. *Mothers of Invention: From the Bra to the Bomb, Forgotten Women and Their Unforgettable Ideas*. Windsor, Calif.: William Morrow, 1989.

Women Inventors and Their Discoveries. Minneapolis, Minn.: Oliver Press, 1993.

Yenne, Bill. *100 Inventions That Shaped World History*. Chicago, Ill.: Bluewood Books, 1994.

The Internet

Surfing the Internet is a fun way to conduct research. The list below provides the Web addresses for sites that will give you some great information on inventors, inventions, inventing, patents, and intellectual property. To find other topics about inventing, use Internet search engines.

Academy of Applied Science: **http://www.aas-world.org**

Benjamin Franklin: **http://home1.gte.net/bowditch/franklin/inv.html**

DaVinci's Inventor Home Page: **http://sulcus.berkeley.edu/Invention**

IBM: **http://www.ibm.com**

Intellectual Property Web Links: **http://www.fplc.edu/**

Invention Convention: **http://inventionconvention.com**

Inventure Place: **http://www.invent.org/**

Lemelson Center: **http://www.si.edu/lemelson/**

Leonardo da Vinci Museum: **http://www.davinci-museum.com**

MIT's Invention Dimension: **http://web.mit.edu/invent/**

National Inventors Hall of Fame: **http://www.invent.org/book/index.html**

The Rube Goldberg Home Page: **http://www.anl.gov/OPA/rube/index.html**

Theta Tau's Rube Goldberg Machine Contest: **http://expert.cc.purdue.edu/~thetatau/RUBE/**

U.S. Copyright Office: **http://www.loc.gov/copyright**

U.S. Patent Bibliographic Database: **http://patents.cnidr.org/**

U.S. Patent and Trademark Office: **http://www.uspto.gov/**

U.S. Patent Documents: **http://townhall.org/patent/patent.html**

Women Inventors Project: **http://www.ccwest.org/french/umbrella/wip.html** or **www.ics.bc.ca/wip**

Surfing the Web

TIM BERNERS-LEE, ENGLISH INVENTOR OF THE WORLD WIDE WEB, ENVISIONED A WAY TO LINK DOCUMENTS ON THE INTERNET USING HYPERTEXT SO USERS COULD GO FROM ONE DOCUMENT TO ANOTHER THROUGH HIGHLIGHTED WORDS. HE DID NOT PATENT HIS INVENTION BECAUSE HE FELT IT WOULD MAKE THE TECHNOLOGY TOO EXPENSIVE TO USE.

The Experts

Part of your research may include talking with inventors and other people, such as scientists, professors, and engineers, who are experts in your area of interest. These people can help you when you get stuck or don't understand something related to your invention. In short, they can clear up questions you may have.

You may even ask one expert or inventor to be your inventor *mentor*. A mentor is someone who can help you develop as an inventor while assisting you with your project. He or she may even let you use special equipment, help you operate complicated equipment, or introduce you to special materials and techniques. All you need to do is contact that person and ask for assistance. If it turns out that he or she cannot assist you, ask him or her to point you to someone who can.

Before you call or write the expert of your choice, prepare a short list of questions you want to ask. Because many professionals are very busy, make your questions brief and to the point. Ask a parent or teacher to help you design your questions.

Check out the following sample telephone interview and sample letter.

The Telephone Interview

Conducting a telephone interview can be easy as long as you are prepared. Here are a few things to keep in mind.

1. Have your inventor's journal and a pen handy to take notes. You should also write down the date, time, and location (if applicable) of the interview. You will need this information when you create your bibliography.

2. Have a calendar nearby. If the person you are calling cannot talk when you call, you can then set up a phone appointment for a later date and time.

3. Before you end the phone call, be sure to get the interviewee's full name and how to spell it so you can send him or her a thank-you letter.

4. Before dialing a long-distance phone number, check with your parents to make sure it is OK to make the call.

Here's a sample interview between a young inventor, whom we will call "Freddie," and Dr. John Hand, an inventor and senior researcher at Bell Laboratories. Freddie is asking Dr. Hand to help him with his invention, a special cane for his handicapped grandfather.

Dr. Hand's office: Good afternoon. This is Bell Labs, Dr. Hand's office. How may I help you?

Freddie: My name is Freddie Knapp. I'm a sixth-grade student at Butterfield Academy in New York City. I'm interested in talking with Dr. Hand about my invention project: a special cane for my handicapped grandfather.

Office: I'll see if Dr. Hand is in. Please wait a moment.

Freddie: Thank you.

Dr. Hand: Hello, this is Dr. Hand, how can I help you?

Freddie: My name is Freddie Knapp. I'm 12 years old and am looking for help with my invention fair project. It's a special cane for my handicapped grandfather.

Dr. Hand: That's interesting. I'd like to help you, but I'm busy right now. Can you call back on Monday around 3:30 P.M.? You can also E-mail me at Jhand@bell-labs.com if you have any questions.

Freddie: Thank you so much. I have three questions I'd like to E-mail you today.

Dr. Hand: You're welcome. Good-bye. I'll be looking for your E-mail.

Freddie: Thank you. Good-bye.

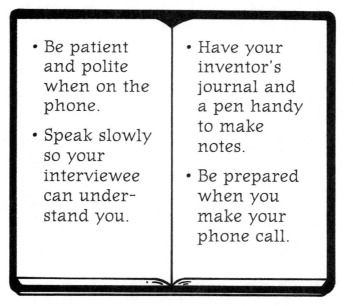

- Be patient and polite when on the phone.
- Speak slowly so your interviewee can understand you.
- Have your inventor's journal and a pen handy to make notes.
- Be prepared when you make your phone call.

The Introductory Letter

You may find it easier to write a letter to your expert rather than to call him or her. That expert may be someone you find while researching your invention in a book or magazine or while surfing the Internet, or may be someone you know personally at a local high school, college, or university.

Be prepared to wait for your reply. After you send your letter, you may not receive an answer for several weeks. You may want to call the person beforehand to let him or her know you're sending a letter and need a speedy reply. Also, suggest a date for him or her to get back to you. You can adjust the sample letter that follows to match your needs.

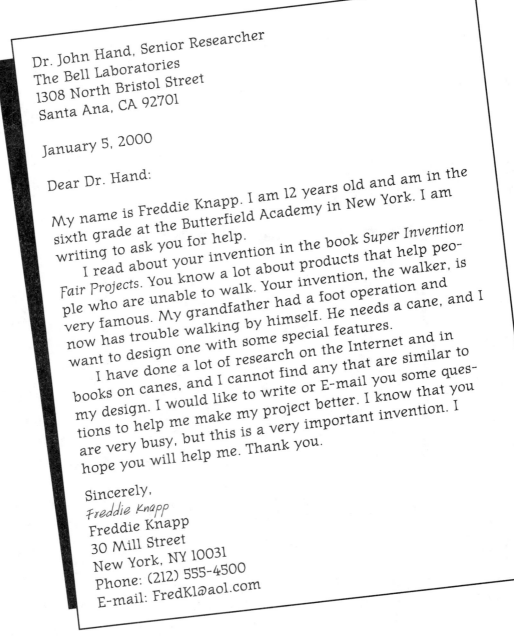

Dr. John Hand, Senior Researcher
The Bell Laboratories
1308 North Bristol Street
Santa Ana, CA 92701

January 5, 2000

Dear Dr. Hand:

My name is Freddie Knapp. I am 12 years old and am in the sixth grade at the Butterfield Academy in New York. I am writing to ask you for help.
I read about your invention in the book *Super Invention Fair Projects*. You know a lot about products that help people who are unable to walk. Your invention, the walker, is very famous. My grandfather had a foot operation and now has trouble walking by himself. He needs a cane, and I want to design one with some special features.
I have done a lot of research on the Internet and in books on canes, and I cannot find any that are similar to my design. I would like to write or E-mail you some questions to help me make my project better. I know that you are very busy, but this is a very important invention. I hope you will help me. Thank you.

Sincerely,
Freddie Knapp
Freddie Knapp
30 Mill Street
New York, NY 10031
Phone: (212) 555-4500
E-mail: FredKl@aol.com

Look at the Superstar Inventor feature on page 53 to discover how Elizabeth Low thought of an imaginative, creative, and inventive product. Before she had a terrific product, Elizabeth researched and experimented.

MEET A SUPERSTAR INVENTOR . . .

Elizabeth Low
Age: 14
Home: Houston, Texas
Invention Name: The Happy Hand
Invention Category: Toy/Display Holder

The Problem: All of the display holders in stores are the same. Why can't there be a fun and interesting holder to display business cards, pictures, or even jewelry?

Elizabeth's Answer: Elizabeth Low, now age 14, wanted to know just that. Together with her sister, Jeanie, who invented a kid's stool, she is the youngest inventor to receive a patent in the United States. Elizabeth noticed that most of the display holders in retail stores are clear plastic shelves or tree-branch holders. None of them were interesting or fun. Elizabeth believed that a holder could be both practical and artistically interesting.

So, she invented a flexible, five-fingered display holder and toy called the Happy Hand. Sometimes she poses the hands on the table to hold her business cards. Other times, she displays kid's rings, bracelets, necklaces, or hair holders. Elizabeth created the Happy Hand with a special orthopedic glove. Before choosing this glove, she tested 200 types of surgical gloves. Most were too flimsy. "Testing gloves means we throw them around, pull on them, stretch them, and see how long they last. The factory—in my garage—can't go into production until I find a glove that outlasts kids," explains Elizabeth.

What a Great Idea!

"I CAN'T THINK OF ANYTHING TO INVENT" IS A COMMON COMPLAINT FROM YOUNG INVENTORS JUST GETTING STARTED ON A PROJECT. HERE ARE SOME MORE INTERESTING IDEAS ABOUT DIFFERENT KINDS OF HOLDERS YOU MIGHT WANT TO TRY INVENTING.

- A DRYING RACK FOR GLOVES
- A SOCK THAT GOES OVER A LEG CAST TO KEEP TOES WARM
- A BELT WITH POCKETS TO HOLD ITEMS FOR SKIERS OR HIKERS
- A DEVICE TO HOLD OBJECTS FOR PEOPLE WHO USE A WALKER OR WHEELCHAIR

Designing Your Project

CHAPTER 6

💡 What is the best way to design my invention?

💡 How complicated should my design be?

💡 What is a subtractive design?

Drawings and Sketches

It is up to you whether you gather your supplies and equipment first and then create your design or create your design and then gather your materials. What is important, however, is that in your inventor's journal you create clear and careful drawings and/or sketches of each design step. Then label each part of your design. Because they keep changing their designs, some inventors make many sketches before drawing a final design. That's normal. It is also normal to add or subtract materials from your original list. Your final diagram will help you decide on your final list of materials. If you eventually have someone manufacture your invention, your labeled journal drawings will show how it looks, what parts it has, and how it works.

Remember the Happy Hand jewelry display invention featured in the previous chapter? Here's how Elizabeth Low had a professional illustrator draw it.

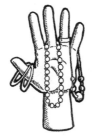  

Subtractive Designs

Your goal is to use the smallest number of materials and parts to get the job done. This will help you create the simplest design, eliminating any unnecessary parts and materials. What is the best way to do this? Inventors think about combining steps. Often one part can take the place of two or three. For example, a popular cup for toddlers has a strawlike mouthpiece. This invention combines two pieces (straw and cup) into one. The cup is easier for the toddler to hold and spills less.

When you make your invention with the smallest amount of necessary materials without losing quality, you have a *subtractive design*. This means you have subtracted from the materials and still have a quality product. Reduced to its most compact design, it's called an *elegant* invention.

What else makes an elegant design? Low cost! Remember that cost is very important. Otherwise, it would be easy to make anything—money would be no object. Therefore, when you design your invention, keep the costs down.

The Real McCoy

ELIJAH McCOY HAD 57 PATENTED INVENTIONS, INCLUDING AN IRONING BOARD, A LAWN SPRINKLER, A SCAFFOLD SUPPORT, A TYPE OF TIRE TREAD, A RUBBER HEEL, AND A CUP FOR ADMINISTERING MEDICINE. HIS MOST FAMOUS INVENTION WAS A LUBRICATOR FOR LOCOMOTIVE CYLINDERS. McCOY WOULD EVEN SEND SPECIAL INSTRUCTIONS WITH HIS INVENTIONS SO NO ONE WOULD GET STUCK WITH A POORLY PERFORMING PRODUCT. BECAUSE OF THIS INVENTOR, WE USE THE SLOGAN "IT'S THE REAL McCOY" FOR PRODUCTS THAT ARE EFFECTIVE AND RELIABLE.

Additive Designs

If you use a lot of materials in your high-quality design, you have an *additive design*. It's easy to fall into the trap of creating an additive design because you think how something would be better if you could just add "this" or "that." But adding new or different features often only results in your product costing more to manufacture. It does not necessarily improve your invention. Plus, your invention becomes less elegant and more *elaborate*.

So, as you invent, look for ways to improve your creations without adding extra parts. Remember to keep your invention as elegant as you can. Keeping your design down to the least possible amount of parts and materials will result in a brilliant, low-cost creation.

—— Try This! ——

WHEN YOU FINISH SKETCHING YOUR FIRST DESIGN, PUT IT ASIDE FOR A WHILE. THEN GO BACK TO IT AND LOOK FOR ANYTHING NONESSENTIAL THAT YOU MIGHT BE ABLE TO ELIMINATE.

Materials, Supplies, and Tools

- What is a junkpile?
- Where can I find materials and supplies?
- What are some common tools I should have?

Your Junkpile

A *junkpile* is a collection of all kinds of "junk," such as toilet paper rolls, soda cans and bottles, aluminum pie tins, milk cartons, or anything else you ordinarily throw away or recycle. Inventors usually have to work with materials that are available. So, it is a good idea to start collecting potential invention materials as soon as possible. That way, when it comes time to begin building your various models, you will have plenty of materials and supplies from which to choose. You might even get ideas on how to best build your invention by sifting through your junkpile!

You can find items for your junkpile in your home or garage. You can also visit your local recycling center to find simple, inexpensive materials. Other good places to find materials are thrift or bargain stores and garage sales.

A *workbench* is a place where tools, supplies, and materials are stored. You will need to create your own workbench when you begin to collect materials and supplies. But, before you choose a place, be sure you have permission to use it.

Below is a list of some common junkpile items you might want to start collecting. Be sure to let your parents know what you are doing so they can help keep a lookout for materials. Also, you will need to find a workbench, or good place to store your junkpile. Your parents may give you permission to use an area of your home or garage, or your teacher may allow you to use part of your classroom.

paper clips	thread spools	paper plates
paper cups	fabric scraps	cardboard
straws	rubber bands	clothespins
magnets	paper bags	string
aluminum foil	plywood	balloons
toilet paper rolls	toothpicks	milk cartons
batteries	pipe cleaners	paper towel rolls
plastic soda bottles	aluminum cans	yarn
film canisters	packing materials	wheels
pulleys	waxed paper	plastic wrap
fishing wire	clay	Play-Doh
egg cartons	hooks	wire hangers
glass jars	rags	metal scraps

Check It Out!

THE FAMOUS INVENTOR GEORGE DE MESTRAL LOVED TO CLIMB MOUNTAINS. DURING HIS HIKES, BURRS AND SEEDS OFTEN GOT STUCK IN HIS SOCKS. ONE DAY, HE LOOKED MORE CLOSELY AT HOW THEY STUCK. HE FOUND THEY HAD TINY HOOKS THAT ATTACHED TO THE FABRIC OF HIS SOCKS. IT WAS THIS OBSERVATION THAT LED HIM TO INVENT THE VERSATILE MATERIAL CALLED VELCRO. THIS "STICKY" MATERIAL HAS MADE A DIFFERENCE IN AUTOMOBILE MANUFACTURING, SPACE TRAVEL, AND EVEN SHOEMAKING.

Keeping Track of Your Materials

You will want to write down in your inventor's journal all the materials you use to build your invention. This includes materials you take from your junkpile and any others you acquire. When it comes time to building your models, make a chart (like the one below) of materials used. It should include the date you purchased or acquired the material, the quantity of the material, and the price. If the material came from your junkpile and did not cost you anything, be sure to note that in your chart as well.

Date:	Quantity - Material:	Price:	Where Purchased:
1. February 2	2 - balsa wood blocks	$1.25 each	Home Depot
2. February 2	4 - strips, PVC pipe (5 ft.)	$.75 each	Ace Hardware
3. February 6	3 - screwdrivers	$1.00 each	Ace Hardware
4. February 9	1 - tube PVC glue	$2.25 each	Model Shop
5. February 12	4 - strips, PVC pipe (5 ft.)	$.75 each	Ace Hardware

Try This!

CHOOSE 10 ITEMS FROM THE JUNKPILE ON THE PREVIOUS PAGE. USE THE ITEMS TO MAKE AS MANY OF THE THINGS LISTED HERE AS YOU CAN IN ONE HOUR.

1. AN INSTRUMENT FOR MEASURING SMALL ITEMS
2. A NEW TOOL
3. A SAFETY DEVICE
4. A CONTAINER FOR RECYCLING TRASH
5. A NEW KIND OF DOORKNOB
6. A SNACK FOOD HOLDER
7. A NEW AND SAFE TOY FOR A SMALL CHILD

SEE HOW EASY IT IS TO TURN YOUR JUNKPILE INTO VALUABLE INVENTION MATERIALS!

MEET A SUPERSTAR INVENTOR . . .

Joel Adam Blondy
Age: 8
Home: Madison, New Jersey
Invention Name: Air Bag Sensor
Invention Category: Transportation

The Problem: Even though they are designed to save lives, many people are killed because of automobile air bags. If a child or a short adult sits in the passenger seat, an inflated air bag can suffocate him or her.

Joel's Answer: "I always wanted to be an inventor and liked inventing things around the house with Legos and pulleys. One day, when we were driving in the car, I brought up the subject of air bags. I thought I could make a better one for kids. I wanted to invent something that would prevent an air bag from inflating when the passenger in the front seat is short.

"First, I thought about doing it with weight, but then I thought that some people might be very light and very tall. I wondered if the sensor on our garage door could work as an air bag sensor. My dad then brought home a Radio Shack magazine for me, and it advertised an even better sensor. I wanted my sensor to detect the height of the person in the seat. So, I used a photo-relay sensor, which has a beam of light that senses how tall the passenger is. If the person in the front seat is too short to break the beam of light, the air bag will not go off if triggered. My invention is made with an infrared photo-relay sensor, air compressor, switch, 12V battery, wires, Kettcar, balloon, and wood. When my dad and I tested the invention to see if it worked, it did!"

What a Great Idea!

HERE ARE SOME MORE IDEAS FOR SAFETY DEVICES TO INVENT.

- A SAFETY DEVICE FOR PETS IN CARS
- A NEW CHILDREN'S CAR SEAT
- A SPECIAL GATE TO LIFT AND STORE WHEELCHAIRS ON CARS AND BUSES
- A PULL-OUT CHAIR SO HANDICAPPED PEOPLE CAN EASILY GET INTO CARS, BUSES, AND TRAINS

Common Supplies and Tools

Your junkpile may contain materials that will become part of your invention, but you still need to gather supplies and tools to put those materials together. Where will you find these tools and supplies? Look around your house—in the kitchen, garage, basement, or shed. Ask teachers at school—especially in the science laboratory and automotive, industrial arts, and technology workshops—if they have any equipment. You do not have to spend a lot of money to get the tools you will need.

Take a look at the list below to get an idea of some of the most commonly used supplies and tools. You might want to begin collecting these. You can borrow or buy any ones you do not have but need for your invention. Store your tools and supplies near your junkpile (at your workbench). Keep them in a special container like a toolbox, shoe box, or lined plastic or wood crate. Keep small items like nuts, bolts, and screws in a paper or plastic egg carton or in small resealable plastic bags.

hammer

drill

electrical wire

clear adhesive tape

hooks/hinges

balance

tape measure

measuring cups

funnels

rubber gloves

tarps

sandpaper

scissors

flashlight

construction paper

pliers

safety saw

nails

duct tape

meter stick

protractor

calculator

buckets

sponges

paper towels

stopwatch

masking tape

rubber cement

stapler

foam board

screwdriver (flat edge and Phillips)

wire cutters

nuts and bolts

screws

ruler

pencil/pen

thermometer

bowls

graduated cylinder

rags

PVC (plastic pipes)

glue

camera with film

hole puncher

Styrofoam

As with your materials, remember to write down in your inventor's journal all the supplies and tools you use. That way, you'll have a record of what you used in case you have to make changes. Also, when your invention is complete, don't forget to return any tools you borrowed.

WARNING!
Working with some equipment can be dangerous. So, when using any power tools, a soldering iron, or a hot glue gun, always ask an adult to supervise. (You will need some of the items when cutting thick or solid materials.)

Scientific Supply Houses

There are no stores or supply houses dedicated specifically to inventions, but scientific supply houses offer many supplies, equipment, and tools perfect for invention making. Look for any local houses in the yellow pages of the telephone book. You can usually find listings under "Scientific Supply Houses" or "Scientific Apparatus and Instruments." Call and ask for their catalogs. Prices will vary from one company to another, so be a careful shopper. Also, make sure you have your parents' permission to make any long-distance calls or order any supplies.

Here are the names and addresses of several popular houses you might want to contact.

Central Scientific Company
3330 Cenco Pkwy.
Franklin Park, IL 60131
Phone: (800) 262-3626

Edmund Scientific Company
101 E. Gloucester Pike
Barrington, NJ 08007-1380
Phone: (690) 547-8880

Fisher Scientific Company
4901 W. LeMoyne St.
Chicago, IL 60651
Phone: (800) 766-7000

Frey Scientific Company
905 Hickory Ln.
Mansfield, OH 44905
Phone: (800) 225-3739

Pitsco
1002 E. Adams
PO Box 1708
Pittsburg, KS 66762-1708

Sargent-Welch Scientific Company
911 Commerce Ct.
Buffalo Grove, IL 60089
Phone: (800) 727-4368

Science Kit/Boreal Labs
777 E. Park Dr.
Tonawanda, NY 14150
Phone: (800) 828-7777

What a Great Idea!

SUPERSTAR INVENTOR DIANA ALVAREZ AND HER CREATION, THE ZIPPER SHOE, ARE FEATURED ON THE COVER OF THIS BOOK. DIANA WON A GOLD MEDAL IN HER SANTA ANA, CALIFORNIA, SCHOOL DISTRICT'S INVENTION FAIR WHEN SHE WAS 13.

THE ZIPPER SHOE IS A SNEAKER WITH A ZIPPERED COMPARTMENT TO HOLD KEYS, LUNCH MONEY, AND OTHER SMALL ITEMS THAT KIDS MIGHT WANT TO KEEP WITH THEM WHILE THEY ARE AT SCHOOL, ESPECIALLY DURING PHYSICAL EDUCATION CLASSES. DIANA'S SIMPLE BUT PRACTICAL INVENTION PROVES THAT "NECESSITY IS THE MOTHER OF INVENTION"!

Building Your Project

- Where should I construct my project?
- What is a "breadboard"?
- How many models should I create?
- What are qualitative and quantitative measuring?

Finding a Workplace

After you've drawn your design in your inventor's journal, you're ready for the next step: building your creation. Find a place at home or at school or elsewhere in your neighborhood to work. (It must be a place where you have permission to tinker around.) Some young inventors have mentors who allow them to work at their place of business, university, or medical lab.

WARNING!
Wearing safety goggles is a must to **protect your eyes** when you take apart and build your invention. Buy them at hardware stores, or order them through a scientific supply house. An apron will **protect your clothing**. You can buy one at a builder's supply store. And always use dangerous tools and chemicals **only under adult supervision**.

Next, if you do not already have one, find or create a special place where you can keep your materials and tools. It can be at home—in the garage, kitchen, or toolshed. Or, it can be at school—in a special place in the science lab or wood shop. Ideally, it should be near your work. Wherever it is, make sure you have permission to use it!

The Stages of Construction
Breadboard

There are three stages of construct- ing an invention. First, you make a quick and easy *bread- board*. This is your first model to test the invention design and show if it really works. It's a simple, inexpensive, and a fast way to see if you're on the right track. You may decide to display your breadboard at the invention fair. Or you might build a model to display.

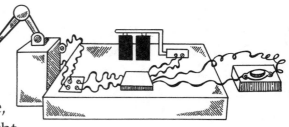

Model

A *model* is the next step in the construction process. It is usually built in order to sell the invention or market it to manufacturers. The model will probably look more like the finished prod- uct. It, too, can be displayed at the invention fair.

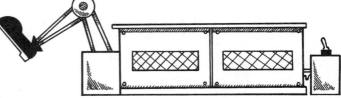

Construction Advice

IF YOU DO NOT WORK WITH A MENTOR WHILE CONSTRUCTING YOUR BREADBOARD, YOU MAY WANT TO ENLIST SOME HELP BEFORE YOU BEGIN TO BUILD YOUR MODEL. ASK A TEACHER OR PARENT FOR SUGGESTIONS. THEY MAY HAVE SOME GOOD IDEAS ABOUT HOW TO BEST MANUFACTURE YOUR MODEL. THEY ALSO MAY KNOW OF SOME PROFESSIONAL ORGANIZATIONS OR CLUBS WITH MEMBERS WHO AS INVENTORS THEMSELVES WOULD BE HAPPY TO GIVE YOU SOME ADVICE. YOUR SCHOOL'S SCIENCE OR INDUSTRIAL ARTS TEACHERS ARE VALUABLE RESOURCES, TOO. JUST REMEMBER, KEEP ACCURATE RECORDS OF THE PEOPLE YOU TALK WITH AND WHAT KIND OF ADVICE THEY PROVIDE.

Prototype

The *prototype* of your invention is a one-of-a-kind sample that looks like and works like the finished product. Manufacturers may make prototypes of your invention in preparation to market and sell it.

Throughout the construction process, you may need to ask someone to cut a piece of wood, bend a plastic tube, or cut a heavy piece of metal. That's fine. You can get help from an adult, your parents or grandparents, or a teacher or adult friend. Still, you should be the one to build each of your models.

Quantitative Measuring

During each stage of construction, you will be measuring pieces and parts. You will use standard measuring tools, such as a scale for weight and a ruler or tape measure for length. This type of measuring, with concrete numbers, is called *quantitative measuring*. The kind of information you obtain is *quantitative data*.

Most of the measurements you make will be quantitative. You will measure length and width, area, volume, weight, and possibly temperature, light, pressure, and thickness. Even when you create your display board for the invention fair, you will use quantitative measurements. You will measure your foam or cardboard backdrop, the colored sheets mounted on its sections, and any platform dimensions. It is important to record in your journal all the measurements of your supplies, breadboard, model, and prototype.

To make a successful invention fair project, you need to know which of the standard measuring tools you should use to get your various measurements. Listed below are a few of the more common measuring tools. (Some were listed in the tools section on page 63.) If you don't have a measuring device you need, ask your parents, science or industrial arts teachers, or an adult friend.

Length and width: ruler, meter or yardstick, tape measure

Area: ruler, meter or yardstick, tape measure, calculator

Weight: balance or scale

Volume: graduated cylinder, measuring cups and spoons, eyedropper
Note: you can also use a plastic soda bottle or milk carton to measure volume. Look on the labels to see how much they hold. If your liquid fills the container, then you know how much you have!

Temperature: thermometer

Light: light meter

Pressure: barometer (atmospheric), bicycle tire gauge (tire)

Thickness: calipers

The Metric System

The *metric system* operates with units such as meters, liters, and grams. Professional inventors and scientists use this system to make all their measurements. It is also the primary measuring system for most countries in the world. The United States, England, and Canada, however, use the *English system of measurement* to make everyday measurements. They only use the metric system for scientific measurements.

You should use the metric system when making all measurements having to do with your invention. To make this easier, the chart below will help you convert from the English system to the metric system.

	Unit	Metric Equivalent	English Equivalent
Length	kilometer (km)	1,000 m	0.62 mil.
	meter (m)	100 cm	1.09 yd./3.28 ft.
	centimeter (cm)	0.01 m	0.394 in.
	millimeter (mm)	0.001 m	0.0039 in.
Mass	kilogram (kg)	1,000 g	2.205 lb.
	gram (g)	1,000 mg	0.035 oz.
Volume	kiloliter (kl)	1,000 l	264.17 gal.
	liter (l)	1,000 ml	1.06 qt.
	milliliter (ml)	0.001 l	0.0034 fl. oz.

Qualitative Measuring

When evaluating something that cannot be measured with a tool, you can instead describe its qualities. For example, if a liquid you are working with changes color, makes noises, gives off a gas, freezes, or boils, you cannot measure that quality with numbers. You will instead describe that characteristic in your journal. This description is a form of *qualitative measuring.* Note, however, that you may be able to give a quantitative measurement to some of the material's characteristics. You can, for example, measure with a thermometer the degree at which the liquid freezes or boils.

Playing It "Safe"

When you build your invention fair project, you'll have to follow some basic safety rules. These rules will not only protect you at your inventor's workbench, but they also will make sure your entry will satisfy invention fair safety standards. Before beginning your project, you should consult the specific rules and guidelines of that fair.

Safety at the Inventor's Workbench

Here are some basic safety tips you should keep in mind while working at your inventor's workbench.

1. Always have a parent or other responsible adult supervise you while you work.

2. Have a fully stocked first-aid kit by your workbench at all times.

3. Be alert and focused while you work. Fooling around may prove dangerous, especially when handling tools and the sharp edges on devices you may be using to build your invention.

4. Wear safety goggles, a laboratory apron, or other special protective clothing when working with dangerous materials or chemicals. Check with an adult to make sure you are properly protected before you start working.

5. Check the labels for special safety precautions before you use any chemicals.

6. Work on a surface that you won't damage. An old wooden workbench or specially treated lab table may work best.

7. Though most electrical projects use 110 volts, they are limited to 500 watts. Remember that a high-voltage source is extremely dangerous. Before working with electrical equipment, get more information on wiring, switches, and metal parts. Protect all wire connections, and always use caution when handling electrical devices. Never have an electrical device near or in water.

8. Never tinker with household power or gas lines.

Invention Fair Regulations

As mentioned earlier, every invention fair has its own rules and regulations about safety. Here are some general guidelines that will help make sure your invention will be accepted into your fair.

1. Table and floor space limitations: Space may vary, so check with your teacher or invention fair director. Usually, a 122-cm (48-inch) wide, three-section, freestanding foam display board, with a height of 91 cm (36 inches) is recommended. Heights up to 182 cm (72 inches) may be allowed if well constructed.

2. Oversized exhibits: Space in the exhibition may be limited, and aisles must not be blocked. Since inventions could be restricted in size, be sure to check the rules and regulations of the fair for approved sizes. If an invention is too big, it may be considered a fire safety hazard.

3. Individual and team projects: Some fairs permit only one inventor per entry. Others allow teams of two or three to enter a single project. Find out your fair's requirements before you ask others to team up with you on a project.

4. "Special" items: Some materials are not allowed at all invention fairs. So, check your invention fair rules before you use any of the following:

- open-celled batteries
- combustible and explosive materials
- syringes, pipettes, and needles
- bacteria, fungi, and molds
- dangerous or poisonous chemicals such as bleach, swimming-pool acid, and ammonia cleaners
- prescription drugs

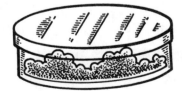

5. Live animals: You should also check the invention fair rules if you plan on experimenting with live animals. Most fairs do not allow experimentation on live vertebrate (with backbone) animals. These include frogs, fish, birds, reptiles, and mammals. You may be able to use invertebrate (without backbone) animals, such as insects, worms, and shelled animals such as crabs. If you get permission to use live animals, make sure they are not harmed in any way. You will also need to fill out all the required forms. If your invention tests human behavior, you may have to complete another special form and have adult supervision.

6. Safety regulations: Each inventor is responsible for the safety of all parts of his or her exhibit. All exhibits must follow county, state, and federal regulations regarding wiring, toxicity, fire hazards, and general safety. Make sure you know all of this information before constructing your invention.

It is very important to have fun while inventing, but please follow the rules, too!

"Safety first!"

is Superstar Inventor Leora H. Saviano's slogan. Read how this award-winning inventor built a safety device for kids and tackled a tough construction problem to win first place at the 1998 National Inventive and Creative Thinking Association's Young Creator's and Inventor's Competition. See page 74.

MEET A SUPERSTAR INVENTOR . . .

Leora H. Saviano
Age: 16
Home: Norwalk, Connecticut
Invention Name: Inflate-a-Gate
Invention Category: Transportation/Safety

The Problem: Each day, millions of children ride school buses to and from school. To protect children who are boarding and exiting the bus from oncoming cars, the bus has flashing lights and stop signs that extend out into the street. However, these safety devices are not enough to prevent all vehicles from speeding past a stopped school bus. Cars and motorcycles pass by in spite of the flashing lights and stop signs. Can there be a device that will physically stop vehicles without damaging them or the barrier?

Leora's Answer: Leora Saviano, age 16, asked that very question. She told us: "I felt there should be a device to prohibit these vehicles from breaking the law and risking the lives of schoolchildren." Leora realized how she might create such a device while she and her family were on a boating trip. Her brother was wearing a windbreaker. He put his arms out in front of him, and the wind inflated his sleeves into two cylindrical tubes. Leora noted this occurrence in her inventor's journal. Later she tried to duplicate the effect with a leaf blower and a small nylon tube. She also talked to her teachers, parents, relatives, and personnel in the school transportation department about her idea to make a better safety device.

Thus, the idea for the Inflate-a-Gate was born. Leora then perfected her idea. She made an air-powered, automatic device with an extending and retracting flexible nylon tube. Leora designed the tube to extend out through a hole in the side of the bus. When activated, the Inflate-a-Gate creates a barricade in the lane next to the school bus. The barrier is flexible, soft, and durable. So, if a car should ever come in contact with it, it won't damage the car or the gate. Leora's creation is an ingenious step beyond warning signs.

Getting Ready for the Fair

CHAPTER 9

- Who will be the judges at the invention fair?
- What should I say at the oral presentation?
- How will my invention be scored?

The Invention Fair

The invention fair is a showcase where you can share your invention with others, as well as receive recognition for your efforts. Whether it is in your own classroom or grade level at school, in a districtwide fair, or at a community site such as a neighborhood mall, your parents, teachers, and the community at large will view your invention. If you are a winner, you can go a step further and receive additional prizes, scholarships, and recognition at one of the many state or national invention competitions. Look in the appendix for a list of invention fairs and special contests you can enter.

— The New Skis —

THE SNOWBOARD WAS THE INVENTION OF
THIRTEEN-YEAR-OLD SKIER TIM SIMS. IT
HAS BECOME ONE OF THE WORLD'S MOST
POPULAR SNOW SPORTS AND HAS EVEN
INSPIRED ITS OWN LINE OF CLOTHING.

The Entry Form

Below is a sample of an entry form. This will give you an idea of the kinds of
questions you'll need to answer when you enter your chosen fair.

Inventor Entry Form

Student Name _____

Grade _____

School _____

Teacher _____

1. Name of invention: _____
_____

2. How did you think of the idea? _____
_____

3. State your problem: _____
_____

4. How does your invention work? _____
_____

5. Whom (your family, friends, pets, the
disabled) does your invention benefit?
_____

6. Why is your invention unique and unusual?
_____
_____

7. Attach your drawings (include
sketches, illustrations, or photos of the
finished model; label all of the parts;
use pen)

8. Attach your inventor's log
(Required when displaying your
invention at a fair. It should be
attached to the display board near the
invention at the actual fair for the
judges to review. You can include
statements like the following: I have
included my inventor's journal to
prove I had the idea first; I filled out
my journal when I worked on my
invention; I initialed and had others
sign as witnesses to verify that I really
thought of the idea and built my
invention.)

The Judges

Your invention will be reviewed and scored by judges. These judges will be people such as teachers, inventors, patent attorneys, manufacturers, and others who are interested in looking at your product and talking to you. If it is a local fair, they will probably be from your community. They will look at your invention, read your inventor's journal, and review your sketches and references. They will make sure they understand how you put together your invention and turned a good idea into a great one!

You might send your invention off to the invention fair to be judged, or you may be asked to stand with your display and give an oral presentation. If this is the case, you may feel nervous and excited. That's natural. Just remember that the judges' questions are not meant to trap or trick you. The judges simply want to understand how you came up with your idea, what problem you set out to solve, how you built your invention, and how it will be used. Be positive and confident. Talk calmly and clearly so that you can be understood. And let your enthusiasm for your invention come through. The more questions the judges ask, the more interested they are!

Judging Forms and Scoring

There are many different kinds of judging forms with different rating scales. In general, judges look for originality and uniqueness. They check to see how complete your journal is; what your sketches, designs, illustrations, photos, and drawings look like; and what research you did. They also want to make sure your invention works as you say it should. Some forms have a total of 50 points, while others have 100. Below is a list (with point totals) of categories that judges commonly consider when judging inventions.

EVALUATION AREAS (POINTS)	WHAT THIS MEANS
1. ORIGINALITY & UNIQUENESS (15 POINTS)	How unique and novel is your invention? Is it creative?
2. USEFULNESS (15 POINTS)	How will your invention be used? Will it benefit a certain group or individual? Is it practical and easy to use?
3. WRITTEN DESCRIPTION (10 POINTS)	How well did you explain how you created your invention?
4. INVENTOR'S LOG (10 POINTS)	Are all your entries dated and witnessed? Did you include everything (brainstorming, ideas, research, supplies list and cost)?
5. INVENTOR'S ENTHUSIASM (5 POINTS)	Did you like creating your invention? Does your enthusiasm come across?
6. RESEARCH CONDUCTED (10 POINTS)	What kind of research did you do (interviews, Internet, reading)?
7. DRAWING (10 POINTS)	Are your drawings clearly labeled and easy to understand?
8. MODEL (15 POINTS)	Is your model well constructed? Does it work properly?
9. DISPLAY (10 POINTS)	Did you make a sturdy display? Is it visually appealing? Did you provide all the necessary information?

On the next page you'll read about a unique and useful invention that won one kid inventor 100 points and first prize at the Tustin Unified School District Invention Fair in Tustin, California.

MEET A SUPERSTAR INVENTOR . . .

Ali Kaslow
Age: 10
Home: Santa Ana, California
Invention Name: The Light Up Purse
Invention Category: Personal

The Problem: "One night, when I was in my mom's car, I wanted to get a piece of gum from her purse. It was dark, and so I had to search for the gum with my hands. But I could not find it. I asked my mom to turn on the car light, but she said she couldn't because it's too dangerous to drive with a light on. I never found the gum."

Ali's Answer: "I thought it would be nice for purses to have lights that could come on when the purse opened. That way, people could see inside them in the dark. I first put a flashlight into the purse, but then realized I would have to find that in the dark, too. And if I put in a big flashlight (which was easier to find), it might make the purse too heavy. Then I thought about inserting a small lightbulb into the bottom of the purse.

"I didn't know how to do that, so I asked my dad if he had any idea how to open the purse and put on the light easily. We went to an electronics store and asked them about my idea. We bought a small lightbulb, wire, magnetic switches, two AA batteries, a battery holder, two small screws, and some tacky strips. I sewed the magnetic switches into the purse, and then connected the wires to the switch. I put the wires through a hole on the battery holder and connected the lightbulb to it. I put the batteries in the holder and put on the tacky strips to hold the purse closed.

"When I tried it, the magnetic switches were backward: When the purse was open, the light turned off, and when it was closed, the light went on! I went back to the store to find a different magnetic switch, one that worked like a switch on a burglar alarm for a window. Then it worked. I wrote everything down in my log and had my dad sign it. I also drew sketches of the two models.

"I next had to find out if there were other lighted purses out there. I went to the mall and looked in all the stores. I called lots of my mom's friends and asked if any of their purses had lights. My next step is to see if anyone else has invented a purse that lights up inside. I would like to get a patent for my invention."

LIGHT

BATTERY PACK

MAGNETIC SWITCHES

TOP OF PURSE

What a Great Idea!

HERE ARE SOME MORE THINGS YOU MIGHT WANT TO TRY INVENTING. THEY WOULD MAKE OUR DAILY LIVES A LOT EASIER.

- A KEY HOLDER THAT OPENS A GARAGE DOOR AND A FRONT DOOR ON VOICE COMMANDS
- BABY DIAPERS THAT DON'T CLOG UP THE TOILET WHEN FLUSHED
- CLOTHES THAT CHANGE TEMPERATURE (WHEN ITS HOT OUTSIDE, THEY COOL YOU DOWN, AND WHEN ITS COLD OUTSIDE, THEY RAISE YOUR BODY TEMPERATURE)
- A NEW WAY TO KEEP PANTS UP

Invention Fair Displays

You will be constructing a visual display to show the judges the steps you took in creating your invention. Every invention fair has its own set of guidelines and criteria, but here are some general tips. Before you build your display, however, be sure to find out the requirements of the fair in which you're participating.

Display Board Construction

Depending on the amount of room you have to spread out, you can present your information on a tabletop or larger, floor display. You can build a display with two panels or three. Generally, older kid inventors build three-paneled displays, while younger inventors use a two-panel file folder to create a display.

Displays usually are required to be freestanding, without the support of any backdrop. Foam board and cardboard can often stand alone, but file folder and poster board displays may need some additional support. If you choose these display materials, you may want to attach lightweight wood frames with hinges so your presentation can stand alone and open or close easily. Whatever style display you decide to use, check the judging guidelines to be sure your display is within the stated size and space limits. Oversized exhibits or exhibits with large floor models are discouraged and may cost you points.

Display Information and Presentation

Though every invention fair has its own requirements, most display boards should include at least the following information: the invention name, the inventor's name, the problem solved, the materials used, a description of the construction process, labeled drawings or diagrams, and a description of how the invention works. Many times, pages of the original journal are replicated and presented as part of the display. Even if you do this, you will need to make your original journal, complete with dated and witnessed entries, labeled drawings, attached photos, research notes, etc., available at the display. Often, journals are attached to display boards with a thick rope or chain. In addition, your invention breadboard or model will accompany your board.

MAKE YOUR DISPLAY BOARD EASY TO READ.

Avoid clutter, and organize your board so it reads from left to right. Your written information should be typed, word processed, or clearly handwritten on clean paper. Stick-on lettering might help your title look bold, as well as neat.

BE ARTISTIC AND CREATIVE.

Use an imaginative border around the display that ties in to the theme of your invention. Also, put colored cardboard or special matting behind your display sheets to make them stand out. You may want to include photos of you building your breadboard. Or you may decide to create some graphs and charts to present some of your research data. If this is your second or third fair, you may add award certificates or medals your invention has already won.

DISPLAY YOUR INVENTION SO THE JUDGES CAN EASILY SEE HOW IT WORKS.

If you create a standing model, make sure you have enough room to show how any moving parts work. If your invention is sitting or lying on the floor, make sure you let the judges know, so it won't be overlooked.

Displaying Your Journal

Adding photos, computer-generated charts, newspaper clippings, written correspondence with experts, and other documents can help make your journal stand out. Just be sure to firmly attach these items to your journal pages (with a stapler or glue) and have them witnessed.

Display Safety

When you set up your invention, keep safety in mind.

- Keep all electrical cords covered.
- Make sure containers are tightly covered.
- Could high or low temperatures affect your invention in any way to make it dangerous? If so, plan accordingly.
- Make sure there are no sharp edges that may hurt someone who picks up your invention to examine how it is built.
- Be sure nails, staples, nuts, bolts, and other assembly parts are attached properly and safely.
- If you use wood, sand down any rough surfaces.
- Check your display for sturdiness. You don't want it to collapse or hurt anyone.

Oral Presentations

You may be asked to present your invention verbally to the judges. This is called an *oral presentation*. Be natural when you give your presentation. Of course, everyone knows how hard it is to appear calm and relaxed when you are nervous and excited. Take a few deep breaths to relax yourself. After all, you've already done all the work. Now comes the best part—you get to tell someone about your wonderful invention.

To prepare for an oral presentation, practice talking about your invention for about two or three minutes in front of a mirror, to your pet, or to a friend or family member. These 20 questions will give you an idea of the type of questions you may be asked.

1. What is special about your invention?

2. How did you come up with the idea for your invention?

3. Did you enjoy making your invention? Why?

4. How long did it take to make your invention?

5. How did you find out if there is already an invention like yours?

6. Is this an original invention?

7. Did you change anything from your first idea? First design?

8. How did you design your breadboard model?

9. Did you put your model together by yourself?

10. Where did you get your supplies?

11. Who helped you?

12. Who were your witnesses?

13. Have you thought about ways to make your invention better? What are they?

14. How does your invention work?

15. Who would use your invention?

16. How can this invention help others?

17. Did you have any problems in the design or fabrication of the invention? Explain how you solved them.

18. How much did your invention cost to make?

19. If you sold your invention, how much would you charge?

20. What else would you like to do to explore your topic?

Certificate of Participation

At the invention fair, every young inventor receives recognition with an official award, called the *Certificate of Participation*. Some inventors are awarded special ribbons and/or educational gifts and scholarships from sponsors.

Remember, everyone is a winner, and every invention is a very special and unique creation.

—— Check It Out! ——

THOMAS EDISON, AMERICA'S MOST FAMOUS INVENTOR, WAS ISSUED 1,099 U.S. PATENTS. BUT HE HAD MANY MORE INVENTIONS THAT WERE NEVER PATENTED AT ALL. HIS SLOGAN WAS "NEVER GIVE UP."

Patents and Trademarks

CHAPTER 10

- 💡 What is a patent?
- 💡 How do I apply for one?
- 💡 What do the symbols ™ and ® mean?

What Is a Patent?

A *patent* is an official document from the United States Patent and Trademark Office (USPTO) in Washington, D.C. It is an agreement between an inventor and society, stating that the inventor gets the right to exclude others from making, using, offering for sale, selling, or importing the invention for a limited period of time. The time period of the agreement varies, depending on the patent. The first person to invent the product or idea gets the patent.

Types of Patents

There are three types of patents currently granted by the USPTO. They include the utility patent, the plant patent, and the design patent. The term of the utility and plant patent is 20 years from the date on which the application was filed in the United States. If the application contains a specific reference to an earlier filed application under patent sections 35 U.S.C.120, 121, or 365(a), the term is 20 years from the filing date of the earliest referenced application. The right extends only throughout the United States and its territories and possessions.

- **The utility patent** includes processes, chemical compositions, and machine manufacture. Most patents fall under this category. Examples might include a new plastic material for the Space Station or a process to clean up oil spills in the ocean.

• **The plant patent** is granted for asexually produced distinct plants and new varieties of plants. Examples might include a new kind of corn or a different-colored rose.

• **The design patent** is given for new, original, and ornamental designs of manufactured articles. The term of a design patent is 14 years from the date of grant. An example might include the design drawings for a new rocket engine.

The Provisional Patent

SINCE JUNE 1995, THE U.S. PATENT AND TRADEMARK OFFICE HAS OFFERED YOUNG INVENTORS A NEW WAY TO FILE FOR A PATENT. INVENTORS YOUNGER THAN 18 YEARS OLD CAN FILE FOR A PROVISIONAL APPLICATION FOR A PATENT WITHOUT A FORMAL CLAIM, OATH, OR DECLARATION, OR ANY PRIOR ART DISCLOSURES. BY FILING FOR A *PROVISIONAL PATENT*, THEY CAN GET AN EARLY AND EFFECTIVE FILING DATE AND CAN USE THE TERM *PATENT PENDING* ON EVERYTHING ASSOCIATED WITH THEIR INVENTION. THE COST OF THE PROVISIONAL PATENT FILING FEE IS $150 FOR A LARGE APPLICATION AND ONLY $75 FOR A SMALL STATEMENT. PAYMENT CAN BE MADE BY CHECK OR MONEY ORDER.

MEET A SUPERSTAR INVENTOR . . .

Trisha Buss
Age: 9
Home: Plainview, Nebraska
Invention Name: The Rubber Back
Suntan Oil Dispenser
Invention Category: Recreation/Medical

The Problem: "I always had trouble putting suntan oil on my back. I also thought about how hard it was to get a good, even suntan on my back. I looked in stores but could never find an applicator that could help."

Trisha's Answer: "I decided to invent something that could apply the oil on my back. I looked for all kinds of materials to put it together. After a while I got a brainstorm. I found some aquarium tubing, a small bottle, and a sponge to start making my first dispenser. When I put all the materials together, my invention didn't work. The aquarium tubing was too flimsy. I looked all over the house and finally found a wooden back-scratcher handle. Putting the tubing on the handle kept it sturdy.

"Here's how it works: I squeeze the bottle, and the oil goes up into the aquarium tubing and down the sponge onto my back. I finished my invention log and drew and labeled the final picture (so I could make it again).

"My Rubber Back Suntan Oil Dispenser won at the invention fair, and I got a computer and a trip to Philadelphia. I'm still working on making it better and getting a patent, but all that takes time."

What a Great Idea!

HERE ARE SOME MORE INTERESTING "SUNNY DAY" IDEAS YOU MIGHT WANT TO TRY INVENTING.

- A NEW TYPE OF FLOTATION DEVICE
- A PAIR OF SUNGLASSES WHOSE LENSES CHANGE COLOR
- SAND SHOES THAT KEEP YOUR FEET FROM GETTING BURNED
- A BETTER BEACH CHAIR
- A DEVICE FOR KEEPING SAND OUT OF THINGS WHILE AT THE BEACH

Filing for a Patent

Here are some basic steps you should follow in filing for a patent. If you want to know more about any of the information provided below, you can call the United States Patent and Trademark Office at (708) 308-4357, or visit their Web site at www.uspto.gov.

1. Do a patent search.

This is a thorough check of the U.S. Patent and Trademark Office's records to make sure your invention is not a duplicate of another, earlier one. You can use the services of an experienced patent attorney to plow through the details and regulations, or you can do it yourself at a patent deposit library. Such libraries are located throughout the country in large metropolitan areas. You can get a list of them from the patent office Web site or by writing:

U. S. Patent and Trademark Office
Crystal Park 3, Ste. 461
Washington, D.C. 20231
Fax: (703) 306-2654

2. Complete a disclosure document.

A disclosure document establishes your right to the patent for your invention if someone else comes up with the same idea before the patent is officially issued. To create your disclosure document, write a description of how your invention works and a statement on its novelty and usefulness, and draw a detailed sketch of it. The document should be on a white 8½" x 11" piece of paper. (You can also obtain a form through the USPTO.) Sign your document, and then send it, along with a money order for $10.00, to:

U.S. Patent and Trademark Office
Box DD
Assistant Commissioner for Patents
Washington, D.C. 20231

Or, for more information, call (703) 308-4357.

3. Write the patent application.

You can obtain a patent application from the USPTO. Because the process can be a complicated one, many people enlist the help of a registered patent attorney. For a list of attorneys, write to:

Superintendent of Documents
PO Box 371954
Pittsburgh, PA 15250-7954

4. Save up those dollars, or find an angel.

The patent process can cost thousands of dollars in legal fees and other expenses. To help with the cost, you may want to find a manufacturer who is interested in making your product and sharing the patent costs. Your patent attorney may be able to help you with this. Or you, your parents, or your friends may know a famous inventor or other investor who would give you a loan or donation. Such a person or company is called an *angel*. Many banks provide loans for new and start-up businesses.

5. Wait for final approval.

The patent process may take up to several years to complete. You can ask other inventors how long it took for their inventions to receive their U.S. Patent Number, the number that proves the patent is registered.

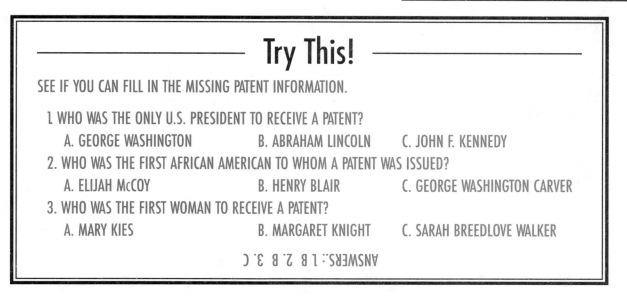

Try This!

SEE IF YOU CAN FILL IN THE MISSING PATENT INFORMATION.

1. WHO WAS THE ONLY U.S. PRESIDENT TO RECEIVE A PATENT?
   A. GEORGE WASHINGTON   B. ABRAHAM LINCOLN   C. JOHN F. KENNEDY
2. WHO WAS THE FIRST AFRICAN AMERICAN TO WHOM A PATENT WAS ISSUED?
   A. ELIJAH McCOY   B. HENRY BLAIR   C. GEORGE WASHINGTON CARVER
3. WHO WAS THE FIRST WOMAN TO RECEIVE A PATENT?
   A. MARY KIES   B. MARGARET KNIGHT   C. SARAH BREEDLOVE WALKER

ANSWERS: 1. B 2. B 3. C

Trademarking Your Name

Many inventors want to protect the name of their invention. They may do this by writing the ™ mark after the name. This mark lets other manufacturers know that this name, or "mark," is being used for a certain product. You do not need to file an application with the USPTO in order to use the ™ mark.

   If you would like to register the name of your invention with the USPTO, you can file an application with that office. If your application is approved, you will be able to use the ® symbol after your invention's name. Many companies and inventors choose to register their company or patented product names with the USPTO. Monopoly®, Xerox®, Reebok®, and Kleenex® are all registered trademark names.

Appendix

Invention Contests and Competitions

After you enter your invention in your school or local invention fair, you may want to find other opportunities for your product. By entering other invention fairs, such as national and international contests, you can win additional recognition, prizes, and scholarships. Your invention may even get "discovered"! It may win a prized place on the U.S. Space Shuttle or gain the backing of a manufacturer interested in helping you build and sell your product. Here are some organizations you can contact for more information.

Annual International Invention
Convention
299 Jefferson Rd.
PO Box 480
Parsippany, NJ 07054-0480

Bayer/NSF Award for Community
Innovation
Christopher Columbus Grant Program
105 Terry Dr., Ste. 120
Newtown, PA 18940-3425
Phone: (800) 291-6020
http://www.nsf.gov/bayer-nsf-award.htm
E-mail: success@edumedia.com

Craftsman/NSTA Young Inventors
Awards Program
National Science Teachers Association
1840 Wilson Blvd.
Arlington, VA 22201-3000
Phone: (888) 494-4994
E-mail: younginventors@nsta.org

Duracell /NSTA Scholarship
Competition
National Science Teachers Association
1840 Wilson Blvd.
Arlington, VA 22201-3000
Phone: (703) 243-7100

ExploraVision Toshiba/NSTA Awards
1840 Wilson Blvd.
Arlington, VA 22201
Phone: (703) 243-7100

Explorers Club
Youth Activity Fund
46 E. 70th St.
New York, NY 10021
Phone: (212) 628-8383

FIRST Robotics Competition
200 Bedford St.
Manchester, NH 03101
Phone: (800) 871-8326
http://www.usfirst.org

International Science & Engineering
Fair
Science Service Inc.
1719 North St. NW
Washington, D.C. 20036
Phone: (202) 785-2255

JETS – TEAMS Competition (JETS Inc.)
National Engineering Design Challenge
Junior Engineering Technical Society
Inc.
1420 King St., Ste. 500
Alexandria, VA 22314-2794
Phone: (703) 548-5387

Lemelson Awards Program Invention
Apprenticeship Program
Lemelson Center
Smithsonian Institution
Washington, D.C. 20560
Phone: (202) 633-8090
http://web.mit.edu/invent/

National Junior Science & Humanities
Symposium
Academy of Applied Science
98 Washington St.
Concord, NH 03001
Phone: (603) 228-4520

Space Science Student Involvement
Competitions
National Science Teachers Association
(NSTA)
1840 Wilson Blvd.
Arlington, VA 22201-3000
Phone: (703) 243-7100

Thomas Alva Edison Regional Science &
Inventors Fairs
c/o Edison Festival of Light
2254 Edwards Dr.
Fort Myers, FL 33901
Phone: (941) 334-2999

Thomas Edison/Max McGraw
Scholarship Program
National Science Supervision
Association
Dr. Kenneth R. Roy, Executive Director
PO Box 380057
East Hartford, CT 06138-0057
Phone: (703) 243-7100

Westinghouse Science Talent Search
Science Service
1719 North St. NW
Washington, D.C. 20036
Phone: (202) 785-2255

Young Game Inventors Contest
U.S. Kids
PO Box 567
Indianapolis, IN 46206

Index

Adolphe, Eric, 15
Alexander, Hattie, 13
Alvarez, Luis, 15
Anderson, Mary, 13
animals, live, 73
Atanasoff, Berry, 10
awards, 86

Bell, Alexander
    Graham, 11, 37
Berners-Lee, Tim, 49
bibliography, 45
Blodgett, Katharine,
    14
books and magazines,
    45–47
Braille, Lewis, 15
breadboard, 67

Carver, George
    Washington, 15
categories, invention,
    26–27
Certificate of
    Participation, 86
construction,
    project
    measuring tools,
        68–70
    rules and regula-
        tions, 72–73
    safety rules,
        70–71
    stages of, 67–68
    workplace for,
        66–67
contests and competi-
    tions, 94–95
Cowlings, Patricia, 14

de Mestral, George,
    59
designs, project,
    55–57
display boards
    construction, 82
    information and
        presentation,
        83–84
    safety rules, 84

Donovan, Marion, 14
Drawbaugh, Daniel,
    37
drawings and sketches,
    55
Drew, Charles, 15

Edison, Thomas, 11,
    86
Elion, Gertrude B., 14
entry forms, 77

Fulton, Robert, 30

Graham, Bette
    Nesmith, 14

Handler, Ruth, 14

innovation, defined,
    10, 18
Internet resources,
    47–48
interviews with
    experts, 24, 43,
    49–52
invention, defined,
    10, 18–19
invention categories,
    26–27
invention fair
    displays, 82–84
    entry forms, 77
    judges, 78
    oral presentations,
        84–86
    recognition, 86
    scoring, 78–79
invention fair
    projects
    categories, 26–27
    definition, 18–19
    design options,
        29–30
    evaluation, 25
    ideas for, 23–24
    invention process,
        19–20
inventors
    characteristics,
        8–9, 13

famous inventions
    and, 11–12
    minority, 13, 15
    women, 13–14

journal, inventor's
    checklist for, 37
    definition, 19,
        31–32
    displaying your, 84
    types of, 32–33
    witness section,
        33–34
judging inventions,
    78
junkpile, 58–59

Kwolek, Stephanie,
    14

magazines and books,
    45–47
Margolin, George, 13
materials, invention,
    58–60
McCoy, Elijah, 56
measuring tools,
    68–70
metric system, 69–70
minority inventors,
    13, 15
models, 67
Morgan, Garrett, 15
Morse, Samuel F., 10

oral presentations,
    84–86
organizations, inven-
    tion, 94–95

patents
    definition, 87
    filing process,
        91–92
    types of, 87–88
planning, project,
    38–40
project ideas
    choosing, 23–24
    design options,
        29–30

evaluating, 25
project timeline,
    38–40
prototype, 68

rating scales, 78–79
registered trademark
    names, 93
research and
    resources
    books and maga-
        zines, 45–47
    definition, 42
    experts, 49–52
    Internet, 47–48
    types of, 43
rules and regulations,
    fair, 72–73

safety rules, 64, 66,
    70–71, 84
scientific supply
    houses, 64–65
scoring, 78–79
Sherman, Patsy, 14
Sholes, C. L., 10
six-week plan, 38–40
sketches and draw-
    ings, 55
space limitations, 72
supplies and tools,
    63–65

team projects, 72
timeline, project,
    38–40
tools and supplies,
    63–65
trademarks, 93

Walker, Madam C. J.,
    15
witness signatures,
    33–34, 37
women inventors,
    13–14
workbench, inven-
    tor's, 58, 71
workplace, 66–67